SPEAKING *of* *Success*

To my Godmother :) —
Thank you so much for always believing in me — Your joy has always motivated me and I hope you enjoy the chapter! —
Next Step Oprah!
XOXO

INSIGHT PUBLISHING
SEVIERVILLE, TENNESSEE

SPEAKING Of Success

Disclaimer: This book is a compilation of ideas from numerous experts who have each contributed a chapter. As such, the views expressed in each chapter are of those who were interviewed and not necessarily of the interviewer or Insight Publishing.

Published by Insight Publishing Company
P.O. Box 4189
Sevierville, Tennessee 37864

10 9 8 7 6 5 4 3 2

Printed in the United States of America

ISBN: 1-60013-067-4

Table of Contents

A Message from the Publisher

When we decided to do a series of books on success, we searched long and hard to find just the right combination of authors who were not only a success in business but were successful in their personal life as well.

The authors we found had personal stories to tell that revealed their inner values—values that contributed to the achievements they have made and the positive influence they have on others. These authors are people whom others revere as persons of integrity. They are winners.

Everyone wants to be a winner. I have never met anyone who wants to be a loser. And I'm sure you haven't either. That's why we found some of the best motivational/inspirational speakers and authors in the country to contribute to this series. Some of these men and women are household names. Others are rising stars. All of them have achieved the kind of success all of us want—the kind that sparks enthusiasm in others and leaves an indelible, positive impression.

The road to success is one of hard work and persistence. *Speaking of Success* can help you unlock your potential and inspire you to realize the many possibilities awaiting you as you learn how to remove any mental blocks you might have to the success you deserve.

If you're already well on your way down the success highway, the stories and experiences of these authors will encourage you, inform you, and I guarantee that you will learn something.

It is with great pride that we Insight Publishing present this series, *Speaking of Success.* We think you will discover that you will find something new each time you read through these books.

The chapters in this series are real page-turners, so get ready to be inspired. Get ready to be delighted. Get ready to learn. And remember, *you* are the author of your own success journey. Others can shine a light on the path but you must do the walking.

Interviews conducted by:
David E. Wright
President, International Speakers Network

Chapter 1

DANNA ANDRUS

THE INTERVIEW

David Wright (Wright)

Danna Andrus is a native New Orleanian, whose seven-year military experiences enable him to understand the need for discipline and structure in the lives of older and younger people.

As a Licensed Marriage and Family Therapist, Mr. Andrus is also a nationally recognized professional trainer, arbitrator, mediator, and urban youth specialist who is able to meet the needs of a fast-paced changing society on all levels. His flexibility, versatility, and fluidity in thought assists him in understanding the complexities of society as he constantly utilizes his unique style to assist in rendering solutions to difficult challenges.

Danna, welcome to *Speaking of Success.*

Danna Andrus (Andrus)

Thank you, David.

Wright

To become successful, why is it not necessary to "reinvent the wheel"?

Andrus

Success is a natural phenomenon. Really, it takes no serious effort on anyone's part to become what he or she was naturally designed to be. The reason success is so difficult for many people to understand or even imagine is because they have been programmed to believe that:

1. Success is only for certain people.
2. To be a success, the price to pay is too great.
3. No one in my family has ever been a success. Why would I be any different?
4. Deep down inside, I am not worthy to be a success.

Success: The Grass Effect

Change your mental programming and success is inevitable. Just as the grass grows, success has to grow. Just as the grass has to be cultivated and trimmed, so also does the individual who is growing into success have to be "cultivated" and "trimmed." Just as the grass may not grow for a season, so does success. Just like the grass magically reappears in season, so does success. Just like the grass is still growing even when it is not in season, it is growing at a level that is not visible to the eye—in its roots. Success is the same way. Where there is a spot in the lawn that is bare, that spot may be barren of grass; someone might come along and plant some grass in that area. The grass comes from somewhere else, but when the grass is planted in with other grass, in time, the implanted grass will catch on the roots of the established grass and will catch on and begin to flourish.

Success in people follows the same process. When you are reading a book, listening to a tape, or viewing a seminar on success, you are taking in information that is being implanted into your brain and connecting with the innate ideas you already have. Before you know it, your season of success takes off. You just needed a little encouragement.

You may look at a beautiful lawn and see a spot on the lawn filled with manure. Repulsive to the eye as it may seem, in time what was once repulsive becomes fertilizer, necessary for the growth and the beauty of the lawn. Likewise, when an individual comes into your life who is trying to stop, block, or deter you from your success, just remember that in time, in the same way the manure turned into food for the grass, that difficult person will turn into what you need. Nothing is bad, only thinking makes it so.

Success: The Wheel/Puzzle Effect

Having read so many books on success, having listened to so many tapes, and having participated in so many seminars, I have come to the conclusion that for an individual to be a success, he or she does not have to invent anything different—or anything that is very different. Success is a wheel that does not have to be reinvented. Success is not a box that is flat on four sides and unmovable. Success is a wheel that keeps on moving, never stopping.

To be a success, all one has to do is grab onto the wheel while it is turning and in time you will be on top. There will be times when you feel like you are on the bottom, but hang on to the wheel—you will be on top again—your turn will come back around.

When you are on the down side, that is where you can attach your spoke of knowledge to the wheel. In time, when the wheel turns again, not only will you be on top, but this time your contribution will be acknowledged.

What I am writing and sharing today is my spoke to the wheel-rolling process. What I may say is already a part of the wheel, I enjoy complementing or enhancing someone else's spoke; I will give them credit. My own humble modes of expertise come with an integration of my least, incorporated with the most, allowing me to be classified as an expert.

Becoming an expert on success came as an epiphany to me. I went through a three-phase process. I was first dependent. I did not know and did not want to know. All I wanted was for someone else to give me some of what they had. Then as I matured, I became independent. I learned and I knew, but unfortunately, a little information can be a dangerous thing. I had become so full of myself that what I knew was not strong enough or even sufficient enough to stand alone.

Eventually I moved into phase three—interdependence. What I had acquired in regard to knowledge, I plugged into life's puzzle, connecting with others. As a result I lost nothing; not only did I gain more, but I was able to see how I fit into the larger picture more clearly than I did when I was a separate piece by myself. I recognized that to be a success, it is not what I knew or could do, it was about integrating that knowledge and skill with what already existed. Another key for me was to feel comfortable knowing that as I became a contributing part of the whole, my personal recognition and contribution was even greater because it fit neatly in the puzzle of life.

When you have an epiphany like that, a new epiphany will come to you that will suggest that every so often the puzzle will require a new piece because the board of life has grown larger. You now have a responsibility to assist others in attaching their piece to the puzzle so that your piece will always be meaningful. Your contribution never shrinks—it only gets larger and more meaningful as others join the puzzle of life. The wheel of success is rolling continuously. Get on board!

Wright

How and why is love for self a necessary perquisite for one to become successful?

Andrus

Success: Knowledge and Love of Self

All of the great teachers of life and all the books of antiquity have made this one statement glaringly clear. So profound is this statement, one would truly have to sit back and marvel at its meaning. The statement is simple and short: know thyself. To be a success, one has to feel good about oneself. A good feeling of success has to start from the inside out.

As an exercise, what I do is to periodically look into the mirror at myself and try to view myself, not as an active participant in the process, but as a spectator in the audience. As a spectator I can see more objectively than I can see up close, subjectively. As a spectator, I can see myself for what I truly am.

The first time I did this exercise I was saddened because I realized I had a lot of work to do. If I wanted more than what the reflection in the mirror was displaying to me I had to do what contemporary writer and motivator John Maxwell stated so clearly in his book, "To get more, one has to first become more." He referred to this situation as "the Law of the Lid." I wanted more. I was not satisfied with where I was because I was not satisfied with who I was. I had become what everyone wanted me to be. Whether their intentions were selfish or laudable, I was still not satisfied—I wanted more. I went to work on myself to be more. I made up my mind I would dare to know my real self.

This is the process I went through: I had to first decide if I really loved myself. I looked up the word "love" and I found out that the definitions ranged from personal and internal to sexual and external. As a result of evaluating and examining the textbook definition, I came up with a formula that works for me. The following is what I came up with. I call it my "Love Formula." Feel free to use my formula or you can create one of your own. All I ask is that you be true with yourself (external) and be true to yourself (internal).

Love means to:

Evolve—When you have the desire to evolve you want to rise to the occasion. Knowing you can evolve means you have the belief that you are more than you have settled to be—you are looking up and you see something that you can and should be. You see yourself as something better. You have an overwhelming desire to want to get there. You are ready to go to work on yourself to become more because you know that is your divine right.

Resolve—Resolve is an energy-charged proclamation that you have made within yourself, that no matter what, you will continue to evolve and to grow. This resolve is the state of being that you feel effectually, now that you are committed to it. It was in your heart and now it's in your head.

Solve—If resolve is the noun or state of your being, "solve" is the action—the verb, the plan of operation—that will assist you in meeting your resolve. You are committed, come hell or high water, to get to that higher state of living, to find that passion of life, to move gallantly and aggressively into your rightful place in life.

Dissolve—This is part one of a two-part action plan that requires work and will. You must first be willing to remove yourself from anyone and/or anything that is not consistent with your greater good. This may be a difficult undertaking because some of the moves you will have to make may require distancing from loved ones who love you dearly, but perhaps their love for you is because of where you are and who you are to them. Selfish as it may be, you have to revisit your map of life and recognize that you have some baggage you must release. That baggage may include people who are dear to you. This can be a painful undertaking; but recognize that if you can stay focused on the objective, then the rest will be taken care of. Because you are in the dissolving process, you do not have to say anything to any of them—you just keep moving forward. They might become angry, but remember, you are moving forward. You are not leaving them but they might just be unable to keep up with you.

Absolve—This is part two of the solution process. You have to take the time to release all the negative energy you have stored up in your being that is blocking you from higher good. The only way you can do this is by purposefully forgiving yourself for thinking and acting in a manner that is less than your higher good. You must be truthful with yourself in this step of the process. Only the truth can make you free. You have a long journey ahead of you. You cannot continue to be weighed down by guilt from the past or anxiety over the future. Release it. As painful as it is, let it go. Your success depends on it—even more importantly, your life depends on it.

This love process—evolve, resolve, solve, dissolve, absolve—is important to understand because once an individual puts it into operation, it can be a painful experience. Realize, however, that *true* love always abounds—it is always there. Love resides in each of the five listed words. Love will never leave you. Love will always find a way.

Wright

Why should one have a clear vision of himself or herself as successful even before the journey begins?

Andrus

Success: Keeping the Vision

To be a success or to be successful, people have to see themselves as already having arrived before they are actually physically there. The only place this can happen is in the only place that can be controlled—the mind. The mind is a powerful thing—better stated: the mind is the power of a person. Whoever controls a person's mind also controls the person. The mind is the center of every individual. Whoever controls the center of a person will control his or her circumference also. When a person has a focused vision he or she cannot perish.

The Bible states that where there is no vision, the people perish (Proverbs 29:18). The mind is the generator that controls the vision that a person has of himself or herself that will, in time, play out as a projection onto the space of existence. My personal definition of vision is "a fixed belief of oneself on the inside in picture form that is projected on the outside in eventual behavior. The behavior on the outside is consistent with the picture one has of the self on the inside."

The controls to the picture one is viewing on the outside cannot be changed from the outside. The control mechanism is the mind. You are in total control of your mind. You can manipulate the controls any way you want to. If you want to be a success, then set your mental controls for success, create the picture of success in your mind and in time it must play out or be projected as consistent with the way you set the controls. Whatever you see on the outside will eventually become consistent with the picture you have on the inside. If the picture on the outside is distorted, it is because you changed the controls. What I have just stated is not a theory—it is a law. As a man thinketh, so is he (see Proverbs 23:7).

The tragedy of this vision—this mental screening process—is that just because people are not aware of it or how the process works does not invalidate the working process and unfortunately, it does not exempt them from the results of the process. This means that the person is not aware of the process, therefore manipulation becomes the order of the day. When people do not have a clear and active vision of working from the inside out, then forces come into play and tell-a-vision (television) happens to them with the controls being manipulated from the outside in. Therefore what they see from the outside becomes a picture of them that was set up by someone or something else. This picture is then taken into their inside and now it will become their vision of themselves and their reality of themselves. What is so fascinating and interesting about the process of tell-a-vision is that it works in the same manner as a mechanical television. You are placed on the desired channel and programmed from the outside to stay there and will only change based on the needs and the interest of the television programmer. That programmer should be *you* and not someone else or circumstances manipulating you.

Now that you are aware of the process, you can manipulate the content whenever you want to. *You* have to make a choice to be empowered or be powerless. You can choose to be empowered from the outside, with someone else controlling your vision, or you can be empowered or power-full (powerful) by creating your own vision of yourself. Just wait, you will be surprised!

Wright

What are four major points people must keep in mind before they begin to embark on their journey toward success?

Andrus

Success: The Journey

When traveling on your journey to success you must remain true to your vision of success. This is so very important because the initial parts of the journey will require a strength that must emanate from the inside. That is why a clear vision is so important. It will become the fuel you will need to stay focused on the outside, even when others do not understand what you are doing and why. It has been my experience that what others do not understand they fear. And if that fear becomes great enough, then those same individuals will tend to do things, even do things to you, that under normal circumstances they would not do.

Here are four steps one must have completed internally before beginning one's journey externally:

Step 1: Make sure this is what you want to do. A mind that is resolute is more precious than gold and it is more dangerous than a nuclear blast.

Step 2: Be aware that there will be people and situations that may not agree with your decision to be successful. Success means change. People prefer that you stay where you are because when you change, you are forcing them to have to change too, at least in the manner in which they deal with you. It's not a lack of appreciation—it's merely laziness.

Step 3: Put distance and time between you and the people you may have to leave behind. And above all, refrain from sharing your ideas of success with everyone. You will find out that on the journey to success, silence is golden. Sometimes sharing your ideas with others while your ideas are still in the embryo stage of development can cause your idea to be aborted or miscarried.

Step 4: Do not look back. If you look back you are going to want to go back. And if you go back, I suggest that you go back to step one of this four-step process. You have to be sure this is what you want to do.

Wright

Name and explain the four procedural steps that every successful person goes through.

Andrus

Success: The Rules of Engagement

From the time I began my career as a professional speaker I recognized that the only way I could get to where I needed to be would involve others. The greater the task, the greater the number of people I had to interact with. I realized I could become nothing great on my own.

Initially what happened was that every time I engaged with others, what started out as something good became a problematic situation for a while. After some changes and some time elapsed, I noticed things began to calm down. Eventually the process continued and I made better progress. What is even more interesting is that every time I had to engage the assistance of others, I found myself going through the same process each time. After a few years of engaging and disengaging with others, I came to the realization that what I was going through was not unique—it was a standard procedure that all successful people and team builders go through. I went through the process of form, storm, norm, perform:

Step 1—Form:

Putting a team together is easy. Keeping the team together is where the difficulty lies. Teams are filled with energy in motion but if all the energy is misdirected or is not moving toward a common cause, the group or team will eventually run into conflict. Every group goes through a "honeymoon" period. The members will show the good you want to see and the good they want you see and the good they think will always be.

A person who is truly success oriented understands the concept of "time." Time will always tell. Time is the greatest tool available to anyone. It will make you, it will break you. Time will tell. In time the truth about anything and anyone will come forth.

Step 2—Storm:

A storm by definition is an attack on a fortified place. The storm period is very valuable to the success process. Living in New Orleans and having survived Hurricane Katrina, I have firsthand knowledge of what a storm can do to you and what it can do for you.

The storm period shows you how strong you are. It shows you what you know and what you do not know. It shows your true character as a person—it shows your resiliency and it shows you where you need to work on yourself. It shows if you have team skills and if you can work well with others. It shows exactly what you are and what you are made of. Such coming out only comes about in a storm or crisis situation.

Just like the storm period brings out the best and worst in you, the same identical process goes on in others also. In the storm process of building, you learn to appreciate that troubled time; it may be a trying and an intense time, but you get through it by deciding to go through it. As with Hurricane Katrina, some people died, some people relocated, some people fell apart emotionally, some people you thought were strong became weak and some people you thought were weak surprised you with strength.

In the storm period you see the best and the worst; in the storm period you will see it all. To be a success and to build a successful team you welcome the storm period because it allows everything to be exposed. You can't fix what you don't know or see.

Step 3—Norm:

In the aftermath of Hurricane Katrina, citizens of the Gulf State areas are looking at what is left and even more importantly, who is left. Now that the contempt and blame game is subsiding, now that the initial shock is over with, now that many are returning to the area after a long period of relocation and dislocation, it is time to rebuild. But in order to do so, rules and legislation have to be put in place that will be stronger and more effective than the ones in effect before. New leadership has to be put in place; a new mindset has to bring in a new order of life—a new way of living. The team is coming together and it is even stronger than before. The storm period is over. The team members who have survived the storm are the ones who are more committed to the process and are going to be a success for having had the experience.

Step 4—Perform:

In one of the books of antiquity, I read a story about a man who went through this same process to get a task completed. Having completed his task successfully, he was awarded the title of "success." So they built the wall, because the people had a mind to work (see Nehemiah 4:6).

A successful person is one who recognizes that greatness is the ability to get more done with more people.

Wright

Why must a person who is going to be successful have an action plan and why must that action plan be S.M.A.R.T.?

Andrus

Success: The Battery Effect

What I have discovered over the years is that life always presents us with something very simple that once explained, the lesson learned can have such a significant impact. I am amazed how geese fly in a standard formation in order to get the maximum effect from their flying. I am also amazed at how ants work together in an orderly fashion to get the job done of collecting food. It also fascinates me how successful people are able to take a simple object and make a lesson in success out of it. I have learned that a person who wants to be successful has to be open, alert, and receptive to everything that is around him or her.

There is always something to be learned. For example, I hear people all the time tell others that when you are on the road to success, you have to be careful of people who will try to hurt you, undermine your efforts, sabotage your endeavors, etc. A weak minded person listening to such a line of thinking would conclude that, if all of this negativity has to do with success, then why would someone want to be a success in the first place? Instead of getting stuck on what others say to me, however, I chose to seek a deeper wisdom that can be extracted from every negative situation.

For example, the battery in the car is what makes the car move in the first place. If there is no battery there can be no movement. We are all walking "batteries" on the move. If we stop it is because we are unplugged. To link to a battery a connection is required to both the positive and the negative terminals. Life is the same way. To be a success one has to experience the negative as well as the positive. Both the good and the bad are all a part of movement. If the negative post is unplugged the car may move for a while but it will eventually stop.

You have to have the negative experiences in your life in order to grow on the move. To never stop growing means to never stop moving. If you are not moving, it is not because of a negative experience—it is because the positive post has been detached. When you stop moving, you are unplugged—you stop growing. On the other hand, if the positive post is unplugged you stop moving altogether. That is why a true successful person always stays positive—he or she knows the negative situations will always be a constant companion. They are not there to tear you down or to give you a hard time; the negative experiences actually validate how strong you really are. If you let the negative get the best of you and you lose your positive energy, then you unplug, not because of the negative but because the positive in you was not strong enough to keep the charge. The positive energy lets you know you are moving; the negative reminds you that you are growing. When you stop because the negative has overwhelmed you, in actuality you have stopped because you are no longer positive about your ability to overcome the negative situation that is causing you to have to grow.

Wright

According to many successful people, why is the knowledge and the understanding of life's master plan so important to individuals who plan to be a true success in life?

Andrus

Success: Solving Problems

I shared a vision of mine with a friend long time ago. I told her that I wanted to win the Nobel Peace Prize one day. She looked at me and tears filled her eyes. For a moment I was rather taken aback. I did not understand why her concern for what I said would cause her to be in tears. What she said to me that day I have never forgotten. She said, "Danna, because I know you are serious about what you just said, I have to ask you, why you would want to do something of that magnitude in the first place?"

I said to her, "I know that in order to win such a prestigious prize I would have to do something large enough that is selfless and that can benefit all of mankind.

"Danna," she replied, "I love you; be ready to suffer."

I didn't give what she said to me much further thought but I did give it due consideration. At any rate, as I sit here today while going through a further exercise of growth, I can say with all confidence that what she told me back then has been evident throughout my professional career even up to today. I have had to suffer much and will continue to suffer even more as I continue on my journey toward success. I want to make it clear that I am not a glutton for punishment; neither do I have a fetish for pain. The pain of suffering that I speak of is the pain of bringing the body under subjection to the rule of my mind that is focused on the prize. Any suffering I experience on the outside is nothing compared to the suffering that I continuously go through to keep my body in line with my mind and my mind in line with my prize. To further understand this concept, these are some of the thoughts that have helped me get through the suffering phase of growth:

1. You determine what it is you want to do. You must also convince yourself why you want to do it. If you do those two things, then you are finished with your part of the process. The "how to" part

is out of your hands. You will see and feel an invisible force of something guiding your every move and every footstep. All you have to do is stay focused and go with the flow.

2. The flow is not always and will not always be smooth, however, it is the path you are to follow.

3. The vision that you have created from within will keep you looking at the end up front so that it becomes your compass pointing to where you are going.

4. Adversity seems also to be a part of the path of progress. Do not be deceived by appearances, but judge each situation with right judgment.

5. What some may mean for evil may be used for good—don't panic, it is part of the plan.

6. Because you understand the battery effect, welcome the negative situations because you know that in the end, growth is your reward.

7. Negative situations are designed to bring out the best in you that would never have to come forth had this situation not occurred.

8. See adversity as a friend and not a foe. When you are able to master that skill, you will be able to destabilize the energy from adversity; you will develop the power to turn adverse energy in your favor ultimately making you more powerful.

9. If thou wilt be good—learn discipline. If thou wilt be better, learn to sacrifice, but if thou wilt be the best, then learn to suffer.

10. All things—circumstances and people—come into your life for a purpose—accept the good and the bad. Place out the welcome mat to greet them since they are coming anyway.

Wright

Why is knowledge and understanding of the "Law of Attraction" and the "Law of Gravitation" important to those who choose to travel the road of success?

Andrus

Success—Working with Law

One thing I found out about success is that it is built on some basic but immutable laws that are consistent with living. According to the dictionary, a law is a sequence of events in nature or in human activities that have been observed to occur with unvarying uniformity under the same conditions. Here are three laws that have assisted me on my path to success:

Law Number 1:

Where you place your attention will determine your intention and will further determine if there is enough for a successful retention.

1. "I am going to be a Nobel Prize winner one day." This is *intention* (noun).
2. "I am writing many books on success and personal growth. I spend countless hours reading and listening to other speakers who are doing the same thing I am doing. I am always looking to give a helping hand to those who are in need. I am investing money in college programs in third world countries overseas that will enable others who are less fortunate to gain a productive education." This where I place my *attention* (verb).
3. "Congratulations! Danna, "Dr. Truth Andrus, is the Nobel Prize recipient for the year 2018." This is the end result—*retention.*

Law Number 2:

The law of gravitation and the law of attraction: whatever is the highest thought in your mind, you will attract and you will gravitate toward situations that are consistent with that thought.

As a success, I have learned to focus on what it is that I want to see and have happen in my life and not on what I do not want to see happen. Along with a clear focus, I then add a clear picture of the end results. I begin to act and believe in response to the end results. With a concentrated focus and clear vision of my already having attained what it is that I want, all things I need begin to come to me as I am also drawn to the things that I need to bring my focus and vision into fruition.

I have profound respect for the manner in which one of the great thinkers of all time has stated this law. He said If I be lifted up from this earth, I'll draw all men unto me (see John 12:32). There is a timeless principle than can be drawn from this statement. Thoughts have drawing power; they can draw us toward whatever it is that we are thinking about or concentrating on at any given time.

Law Number 3:

Whatever you want, be willing to help others get what they want. Give and you shall receive.

Since I have practiced this law, I have acquired great success. What I do is state clearly what it is that I want. With confidence I commit myself to the belief that in time I shall receive it. Next, I unselfishly begin to help others get what they want. What happens at this point is where the law begins. As I extend myself to others, I am stretching myself even more while in the extension process. The more people I help, the more I extend and the more I am stretched. What happens now is that the area I once had has changed and is larger now in breadth, in width, in height, and in depth. If I were to see myself as a container, then by assisting others I have enlarged my container. The more people I help, the more I stretch and am stretched. My container becomes as large and is equivalent to the number of people I assist. For my earlier request to be received and fulfilled, the universe has to fill the request based on my current area and space. What I finally receive is much more than I asked for because the space for me to receive it is much larger. If this law is correct and irrefutable as I know it to be, let me try another experiment.

I am purposely setting this law in motion. I am thankful for the blessings that I am receiving for having invested myself, my time, and my income to being a contributing writer to this book, *Speaking of Success*. I am so confident of the blessing I am receiving that I am giving thanks right now as I envision myself daily going to the bank to make huge deposits from the sales of this book. I am attending workshops and seminars talking about the impact of this book. I am humbly saying yes to the many offers I am receiving to be keynote speaker at conferences all around the country and the world. In my presentations I am referring my audiences to *Speaking of Success* as a guide for living successfully.

I am thankful that this book is assisting me in becoming a great success as well as a world-class expert on the subject of success. I am thankful and I bless all the people who have blessed me to become a greater blessing to others. Even now as I write this passage, I envision this book in its twelfth printing. I am receiving contracts from all over the world because of what other authors and I have written in this book. This book is helping millions to be encouraged about their lives. I am thankful that millions have been blessed because of my literary contribution.

And it will come to pass that my initial request will be fulfilled. I am not the same person I was when I made the initial request and neither is my container. As a great biblical King once put it, ". . . my cup runneth over" (Psalm 23:5b). I am a millionaire! And just think, this book has not even been published yet! (See you all on the *Oprah* show!)

Wright

What are some of the wise saying you know that will act as fuel for my mental engine that provides me with the resiliency and energetic lift I need to keep going when I am detained, distracted, denied, or just want to give up?

Andrus

Success: Never Forget Your Foundation.

Success is never forgetting the many people and situations that contributed to making you the person you have become. Many people and situations both good and bad have positioned me to get closer to my ultimate prize—the Nobel Peace Prize. I am convinced that all I have gone through was necessary for me to become who I am today and who I shall be in the future. Many people slaved laboriously with me to get me to this point of professional maturity where I can dare be called a success and a world-class expert in the field.

My children, Danna II and Shi'Mere have been a great support to me. Their eldest sister, Sha'Ellen, who I am blessed to have raised as a single parent for the last twenty-nine years, is truly my greatest joy. Sha'Ellen is challenged and nonverbal, but over the years she has said more to me in silence than any others could have tried to say in words. She is the main reason I am a success today.

The beginning Pillars of TRUTHLINK 2150, Inc, the organization that has produced the nationally acclaimed youth program D.E.P.U.T.Y. (Direct Effective Positive Uplifting of Today's Youth), I can never forget. One person (I will not mention her name, but she knows who she is) in her own way has kept up with my progress. To her I say, "Through many dangers toils and snares, I have already come." And to her I say, "Thank you." To the other pillar, Tina Marie Simpson now residing Dallas, Texas, thank you. It actually took a storm to break us apart. But in actuality, we are so tied together that no matter what, you will always be the "T" in truth—both in the beginning and at the end of the word. Tina did what no other person dared to do—she trusted and believed in me when no one else would. For that reason she has been given the greatest honor one can bestow on another—she is called a "friend." And then to my mother, Golden Andrus, who made this all possible, thanks for taking time to make yourself available to bring me forth so I can be here. And to my father, Jesse Lee Andrus Sr., who is smiling down on me, I have kept your words true, "Wisdom walks before the time, opportunity walks with the time, and only regrets and remorse walk after the time." You said, "Son, this is the time to get thee some wisdom," and it looks like I did.

Conclusion

I do not know quite how to end this part of my contribution to this book so I will do it in story form. I will take a short story from the Bible that will convey every thought, idea, principle, and message that I have tried to cover in these last pages. I am not trying to sound religious—just trying to make a point.

Once upon a time there were five wise virgins and five foolish virgins. The five wise virgins were always busy trimming the wicks in their lamps and making sure their lamps stayed filled with oil. Each day, month in and month out, the five wise virgins followed this routine. They knew that their work would not be in vain.

The five foolish virgins, on the other hand, each day would laugh and mock the other five virgins. They would tell them, "You are crazy for doing the same tasks over and over again." The foolish said to the wise, "There will never be a need for you to use those lamps; you are only wasting time." The five virgins continued to ignore the foolish virgins as they continued about their routine. The foolish girls continued to laugh and mock the wise.

One day, in the middle of the night, the bridegroom they were waiting for came. The five wise virgins arose, took their prepared lamps, lit their wicks, and began to make their way to the place where the marriage dinner party would be held. The five foolish girls, puzzled and startled, began to panic because here was their opportunity to meet the bridegroom also, however, they had no oil in their lamps. As a last resort, they hurried to their wise counterparts and begged them to share their oil. The five wise virgins said to them, "No we can't share our oil, lest there be not enough for us and you. But go rather to those who sell and buy for yourselves." The five foolish girls left sadly into the night. When they returned they were too late. The door was shut and the guardian of the door did not know them. (From Matthew 25:1–13.)

Someone reading this story is probably thinking that the five foolish virgins deserved their plight but maybe the wise girls should have shared with them. That argument would be a good one if the story at all levels was restricted to oil and lamps. But a deeper wisdom is that the story was about more than oil and lamps. You can give someone your money, you can give someone your car, and you can give someone your advice. But one thing you cannot give another is your preparedness. Success is about being prepared. I am preparing myself each day, are you?

About the Author

Danna Andrus is a native New Orleanian and a military veteran. His educational experiences include completing his associate degree, bachelor's degree, and he earned a Master of Arts degree in Education: Marriage and Family Therapy from Our Lady of Holy Cross College. Currently, Mr. Andrus is a Licensed Marriage and Family Therapist and a member of the National Speakers Association. His flexibility, versatility, and fluidity in thought assists and aids him in understanding the complexities of society.

Danna "Dr. TRUTH" Andrus
TRUTHLINK 2150, Inc.
P.O. Box 741712
New Orleans, LA 70114
Phone: 504.416.5256
Fax: 504.341.6650
E-mail: itruth21st@aol.com
www.truthlink2150.com

Chapter 2

DR. STEPHEN R. COVEY

THE INTERVIEW

David Wright (Wright)

We're talking today with Dr. Stephen R. Covey, cofounder and vice-chairman of Franklin Covey Company, the largest management company and leadership development organization in the world. Dr. Covey is perhaps best known as the author of *The 7 Habits of Highly Effective People* which is ranked as a number one best seller by the *New York Times*, having sold more than fourteen million copies in thirty-eight languages throughout the world. Dr. Covey is an internationally respected leadership authority, family expert, teacher, and organizational consultant. He has made teaching principle-centered living and principle-centered leadership his life's work. Dr. Covey is the recipient of the Thomas More College Medallion for Continuing Service to Humanity and has been awarded four honorary doctorate degrees. Other awards given Dr. Covey include the Sikh's 1989 International Man of Peace award, the 1994 International Entrepreneur of the Year award, *Inc. magazine's* Services Entrepreneur of the Year award, and in 1996 the National Entrepreneur of the Year Lifetime Achievement award for Entrepreneurial leadership. He has also been recognized as one of *Time Magazine's* twenty-five most influential Americans and one of

Sales and Marketing Management's top twenty-five power brokers. Dr. Covey earned his undergraduate degree from the University of Utah, his MBA from Harvard, and completed his doctorate at Brigham Young University. While at Brigham Young he served as assistant to the President and was also a professor of business management and organizational behavior. Dr. Covey, welcome to *Speaking of Success!*

Dr. Stephen Covey (Covey)

Thank you.

Wright

Dr. Covey, most companies make decisions and filter them down through their organization. You, however, state that no company can succeed until individuals within it succeed. Are the goals of the company the result of the combined goals of the individuals?

Covey

Absolutely, because if people aren't on the same page they're going to be pulling in different directions. To teach this concept, I frequently ask large audiences to close their eyes and point north, and then to keep pointing and open their eyes and they find themselves pointing all over the place. I say to them, "Tomorrow morning if you want a similar experience, ask the first ten people you meet in your organization what the purpose of your organization is and you'll find it's a very similar experience. They'll point all over the place." When people have a different sense of purpose and values, every decision that is made from then on is governed by those. There's no question that this is one of the fundamental causes of misalignment, low trust, interpersonal conflict, interdepartmental rivalry, people operating on personal agendas, and so forth.

Wright

Is that mostly a result of the inability to communicate from the top?

Covey

That's one aspect, but I think it's more fundamental. There's an inability to involve people—an unwillingness. Leaders may communicate what their mission and their strategy is, but that doesn't mean there's any emotional connection to it. Mission statements that are rushed and then announced are soon forgotten. They become nothing more than just a bunch of platitudes on the wall that mean essentially nothing and even create a source of cynicism and a sense of hypocrisy inside the culture of an organization.

Wright

How do companies ensure survival and prosperity in these tumultuous times of technological advances, mergers, downsizing, and change?

Covey

I think that it takes a lot of high trust in a culture that has something that doesn't change—principles—at its core. There are principles that people agree upon that are valued. It gives a sense of stability. Then you have the power to adapt and be flexible when you experience these kinds of disruptive new economic models or technologies that come in and sideswipe you. You don't know how to handle them unless you have something you can depend upon. If people have not agreed to a common set of principles that guide them and a common purpose, then they get their security from the outside and they tend to freeze the structure, systems, and processes inside and they cease becoming adaptable. They don't change with the changing realities of the new marketplace out there and gradually they become obsolete.

Wright

I was interested in one portion of your book *The 7 Habits of Highly Effective People* where you talk about behaviors. How does an individual go about the process of replacing ineffective behaviors with effective ones?

Covey

I think that for most people it usually requires a crisis that humbles them to become aware of their ineffective behaviors. If there's not a crisis the tendency is to perpetuate those behaviors and not change. You don't have to wait until the marketplace creates the crisis for you. Have everyone accountable on a 360 degree basis to everyone else they interact with—with feedback either formal or informal—where they are getting data as to what's happening. They will then start to realize that the consequences of their ineffective behavior require them to be humble enough to look at that behavior and to adopt new, more effective ways of doing things. Sometimes people can be stirred up to this if you just appeal to their conscience—to their inward sense of what is right and wrong. A lot of people sometimes know inwardly they're doing wrong, but the culture doesn't necessarily discourage them from continuing that. They either need feedback from people, or they need feedback from the marketplace, or they need feedback from their conscience. Then they can begin to develop a step-by-step process of replacing old habits with new, better habits.

Wright

It's almost like saying, "Let's make all the mistakes in the laboratory before we put this thing in the air."

Covey

Right; and I also think what is necessary is a paradigm shift, which is analogous to having a correct map, say of a city or of a country. If people have an inaccurate paradigm of life, of other people, and of themselves it really doesn't make much difference what their behavior or habits or attitudes are. What they need is a correct paradigm—a correct map—that describes what's going on. For instance, in the Middle Ages they used to heal people through bloodletting. It wasn't until Samuel Weiss and Pasteur and other empirical scientists discovered the germ theory that they realized for the first time they weren't dealing with the real issue. They realized why women preferred to use midwives who washed rather than doctors who didn't wash. They gradually got a new paradigm. Once you've got a new paradigm then your behavior and your attitude flows directly from it. If you have a bad paradigm or a bad map, let's say of a city, there's no way, no matter what your behavior or your habits or your attitudes are—how positive they are—you'll never be able to find the location you're looking for. This is why I believe that to change paradigms is far more fundamental than to work on attitude and behavior.

Wright

One of your seven habits of highly effective people is to begin with the end in mind. If circumstances change and hardships or miscalculation occurs, how does one view the end with clarity?

Covey

Many people think to begin with the end in mind means that you have some fixed definition of a goal that's accomplished and if changes come about you're not going to adapt to them. Instead, the "end in mind" you begin with is that you are going to create a flexible culture of high trust so that no matter what comes along you are going to do whatever it takes to accommodate that new change or that new reality and maintain a culture of high performance and high trust. You're talking more in terms of values and overall purposes which don't change, rather than specific strategies or programs that will have to change to accommodate the changing realities in the marketplace.

Wright

In this time of mistrust between people, corporations, and nations for that matter, how do we create high levels of trust?

Covey

That's a great question and it's complicated because there are so many elements that go into the creating of a culture of trust. Obviously the most fundamental one is just to have trustworthy people. But that is not sufficient because what if the organization itself is misaligned? For instance, what if you say you value cooperation but you really reward people for internal competition? Then you have a systemic or a structure problem that creates low trust inside the culture even though the people themselves are trustworthy. This is one of the insights of Edward Demming and the work he did. That's why he said that most problems are not personal; they're systemic. They're common caused. That's why you have to work on structure, systems, and processes to make sure that they institutionalize principle-centered values. Otherwise you could have good people with bad systems and you'll get bad results.

When it comes to developing interpersonal trust between people, it is made up of many, many elements such as taking the time to listen to other people, to understand them, and to see what is important to them. What we think is important to another may only be important to us, not to another. It takes empathy. You have to make and keep promises to them. You have to treat them with kindness and courtesy. You have to be completely honest and open. You have to live up to your commitments. You can't betray them behind their back. You can't badmouth them behind their back and sweet-talk them to their face. That will send out vibes of hypocrisy and it will be detected. You have to learn to apologize when you make mistakes, to admit mistakes, and to also get feedback going in every direction as much as possible. It doesn't necessarily require formal forums; it requires trust between people that will be open with each other and give each other feedback.

Wright

My mother told me to do a lot of what you're saying now, but it seems like when I got in business I simply forgot.

Covey

Sometimes we forget, but sometimes culture doesn't nurture it. That's why I say unless you work with the institutionalizing—that means formalizing into structure, systems, and processes the values—you will not have a nurturing culture. You have to constantly work on that. This is one of the big mistakes organizations make. They think trust is simply a function of being honest. That's only one small aspect. It's an important aspect, obviously, but there are so many other elements that go into the creation of a high trust culture.

Wright

"Seek first to understand then to be understood" is another of your seven habits. Do you find that people try to communicate without really understanding what other people want?

Covey

Absolutely. The tendency is to project out of our own autobiography—our own life, our own value system—onto other people, thinking we know what they want. So we don't really listen to them. We pretend to listen, but we really don't listen from within their frame of reference. We listen from within our own frame of reference and we're really preparing our reply rather than seeking to understand. This is a very common thing. In fact very few people have had any training in seriously listening. They're trained in how to read, write, and speak, but not to listen.

Reading, writing, speaking, and listening are the four modes of communication and they represent about two-thirds to three-fourths of our waking hours. About half of that time is spent listening, but it's the one skill people have not been trained in. People have had all this training in the other forms of communication. In a large audience of

1,000 people you wouldn't have more than twenty people who have had more than two weeks of training in listening. Listening is more than a skill or a technique so that you're listening within another frame of reference. It takes tremendous courage to listen because you're at risk when you listen. You don't know what's going to happen; you're vulnerable.

Wright

Sales gurus always tell me that the number one skill in selling is listening.

Covey

Yes—listening from within the customer's frame of reference. That is so true. You can see that it takes some security to do that because you don't know what's going to happen.

Wright

With our *Speaking of Success!* talk show and book we're trying to encourage people in our audience to be better, to live better, and be more fulfilled by listening to the examples of our guests. Is there anything or anyone in your life that has made a difference for you and helped you to become a better person?

Covey

I think the most influential people in my life have been my parents. I think that what they modeled was not to make comparisons and harbor jealousy or to seek recognition. They were humble people. I remember my mother one time when we were going up in an elevator and the most prominent person in the state was in the elevator. She knew him, but she spent her time talking to the elevator operator. I was just a little kid and I was so awed by this person and I said to my mom, "Why didn't you talk to the important person?" She said, "I was. I had never met him." They were really humble, modest people who were focused on service and other people rather than on themselves. I think they were very inspiring models to me.

Wright

In almost every research paper that anyone I've ever read writes about people who influenced their lives, in the top five people, three of them are teachers. My seventh grade English teacher was the greatest teacher I ever had and influenced me to no end.

Covey

Would it be correct to say that she saw in you probably some qualities of greatness you didn't even see in yourself?

Wright

Absolutely.

Covey

That's been my general experience that the key aspect of a mentor or a teacher is someone who sees in you potential that you don't even see in yourself. They treat you accordingly and eventually you come to see it in yourself. That's my definition of leadership or influence—communicating people's worth and potential so clearly that they are inspired to see it in themselves.

Wright

Most of my teachers treated me as a student, but she treated me with much more respect than that. As a matter of fact, she called me Mr. Wright in the seventh grade. I'd never been addressed by anything but a nickname. I stood a little taller; she just made a tremendous difference. Do you think there are other characteristics that mentors seem to have in common?

Covey

I think they are first of all good examples in their own personal lives. Their personal lives and their family lives are not all messed up—they come from a base of good character. They also are usually very confident and they take the time to do what your teacher did to you—to treat you with uncommon respect and courtesy.

They also, I think, explicitly teach principles rather than practices so that rules don't take the place of human judgment. You gradually come to have faith in your own judgment in making decisions because of the affirmation of such a mentor. Good mentors care about you—you can feel the sincerity of their caring. It's like the expression, "I don't care how much you know until I know how much you care."

Wright

Most people are fascinated with the new television shows about being a survivor. What has been the greatest comeback that you've made from adversity in your career or your life?

Covey

When I was in grade school I experienced a disease in my legs. It caused me to use crutches for a while. I tried to get off them fast and get back. The disease wasn't corrected yet so I went back on crutches for another year. The disease went to the other leg and I went on for another year. It essentially took me out of my favorite thing—athletics—and it took me more into being a student. So that was kind of a life-defining experience which at the time seemed very negative, but has proven to be the basis on which I've focused my life—being more of a learner.

Wright

Principle-centered learning is basically what you do that's different from anybody I've read or listened to.

Covey

The concept is embodied in the far-eastern expression, "Give a man a fish, you feed him for the day; teach him how to fish, you feed him for a lifetime." When you teach principles that are universal and timeless, they don't belong to just any one person's religion or to a particular culture or geography. They seem to be timeless and universal like the ones we've been talking about here: trustworthiness, honesty, caring, service, growth, and development. These are universal principles. If you focus on these things then little by little people become independent of you and then they start to believe in themselves and their own judgment becomes better. You don't need as many rules. You don't need as much bureaucracy and as many controls and you can empower people.

The problem in most business operations today—and not just business but non-business—is that they're using the industrial model in an information age. Arnold Toynbee, the great historian, said, "You can pretty well summarize all of history in four words: nothing fails like success." The industrial model was based on the asset of the machine. The information model is based on the asset of the person—the knowledge worker. It's an altogether different model. But the machine model was the main asset of the twentieth century. It enabled productivity to increase fifty times. The new asset is intellectual and social capital—the qualities of people and the quality of the relationship they have with each other. Like Toynbee said, "Nothing fails like success." The industrial model does not work in an information age. It requires a focus on the new wealth, not capital and material things.

A good illustration that demonstrates how much we were into the industrial model, and still are, is to notice where people are on the balance sheet. They're not found there. Machines are found there. Machines become investments. People are on the profit and loss statement and people are expenses. Think of that; if that isn't bloodletting.

Wright

It sure is.

When you consider the choices you've made down through the years, has faith played an important role in your life?

Covey

It has played an extremely important role. I believe deeply that we should put principles at the center of our lives, but I believe that God is the source of those principles. I did not invent them. I get credit sometimes for some of the Seven Habits material and some of the other things I've done, but it's really all based on principles that have been given by God to all of His children from the beginning of time. You'll find that you can teach these same principles from the sacred texts and the wisdom literature of almost any tradition. I think the ultimate source of that is God and that is one thing you can absolutely depend upon—in God we trust.

Wright

If you could have a platform and tell our audience something you feel would help them or encourage them, what would you say?

Covey

I think I would say to put God at the center of your life and then prioritize your family. No one on their deathbed ever wished they spent more time at the office.

Wright

That's right. We have come down to the end of our program and I know you're a busy person, but I could talk with you all day Dr. Covey.

Covey

It's good to talk with you as well and to be a part of this program. It looks like an excellent one that you've got going on here.

Wright

Thank you.

We have been talking today with Dr. Stephen R. Covey, co-founder and vice-chairman of Franklin Covey Company. He's also the author of *The 7 Habits of Highly Effective People,* which has been ranked as a number one bestseller by the *New York Times*, selling more than fourteen million copies in thirty-eight languages.

Dr. Covey, thank you so much for being with us today on *Speaking of Success!*

Covey

Thank you for the honor of participating.

About The Author

In 1996, Stephen R. Covey was recognized as one of Time magazine's twenty-five most influential Americans and one of Sales and Marketing Management's top twenty-five power brokers. Dr. Covey is the author of several acclaimed books, including the international bestseller, *The 7 Habits of Highly Effective People*. It has sold more than fifteen million copies in thirty-eight languages throughout the world. Other bestsellers authored by Dr. Covey include *First Things First, Principle-Centered Leadership*, with sales exceeding one million, and *The 7 Habits of Highly Effective Families.*

Dr. Covey's newest book, *The 8th Habit: From Effectiveness to Greatness*, which was released in November 2004, has risen to the top of several bestseller lists, including *New York Times, Wall Street Journal, USA Today Money, Business Week*, and Amazon.com and Barnes & Noble. The 8th Habit has sold more than 360,000 copies.

Dr. Covey earned his undergraduate degree from the University of Utah, his MBA from Harvard, and completed his doctorate at Brigham Young University. While at Brigham Young University, he served as assistant to the president and was also a professor of business management and organizational behavior. He received the National Fatherhood Award in 2003, which, as the father of nine and grandfather of forty-four, he says is the most meaningful award he has ever received.

Dr. Covey currently serves on the board of directors for the Points of Light Foundation. Based in Washington, D.C., the Foundation, through its partnership with the Volunteer Center National Network, engages and mobilizes millions of volunteers from all walks of life—businesses, nonprofits, faith-based organizations, low-income communities, families, youth, and older adults—to help solve serious social problems in thousands of communities.

Dr. Stephen R. Covey
www.stephencovey.com

Chapter 3

ANNAROSE INGARRA-MILCH AND CHARLES MILCH

THE INTERVIEW

David Wright (Wright)

Today we are speaking with coprenuers Annarose Ingarra-Milch and Charles Milch. They own ROI Training & Consulting (ROI), a mission-driven, employee development and management consulting firm dedicated to helping clients achieve success. Whether advising organizations on core strategy or facilitating tailor-made, critical skills training programs, Annarose and Charles emphasize that successful businesses are built on successful relationships.

Annarose and Charles partner with each client to share their combined fifty years of corporate experience—Charles as a CEO in the health and service industry and Annarose as a businesswoman and corporate trainer.

Together they tap their synergetic relationship and natural dual perspective to challenge organizations to maximize their workforce, workplace, and systems relationships.

Using a blend of their real life stories and humorous anecdotes, Annarose and Charles deliver high energy training and keynote presentations designed to engage and motivate audiences.

Charles and Annarose welcome to *Speaking of Success.*

Charles Milch (Charles)

Thank you, David.

Annarose Ingarra-Milch (Annarose)

Thank you, David.

Wright

You refer to yourselves as "coprenuers." It is a term we do not hear every day. Tell me about coprenuers?

Charles

David, coprenuers are entrepreneurial couples who work together as equal partners in the company. The National Federation of Independent Business estimates that there are more than 1 million of us husband-and-wife teams running companies in the United States.

Annarose

In fact, David, recently I read that companies co-owned by spouses represent one of the fastest growing business sectors.

Wright

Sounds like a "mom and pop" business. Is there a difference between traditional "mom and pop" businesses and coprenuers?

Annarose

Traditional mom and pop businesses have one partner as a "boss" and the other acts as a "subordinate." Charles and my immigrant grandparents each owned small, neighborhood grocery stores. In both instances, Grandpa was the boss and Grandma did what Grandpa told her (at least during business hours).

Charles

Coprenuers operate differently. They view themselves as equal partners—each one capitalizing on their strengths and skills to manage the business. At ROI, Annarose and I share all the responsibilities based on each of our capabilities.

Wright

How did you decide you could be successful working together?

Annarose

David, Charles and I have been married for almost thirty years. We have a strong personal relationship. We value each other. We enjoy each other's company. We support each other's goals. And we share a clear vision of our life together. These are important ingredients for a successful relationship.

In the beginning of our marriage, Charles and I were like many young couples, caring for our children while building our individual careers. Throughout the years we imagined and discussed what we wanted our future to look like. Both of us visualized working side-by-side as a team. Owning a business together became our goal. We had confidence our successful personal relationship would transfer into a successful business relationship. Credit Stephen R. Covey, as we "began with the end in mind."

When it was time to turn our dream into our reality, we put pen to paper and very specifically outlined what we wanted to achieve. Together we designed our goals. The goal-planning process required us to take an inventory of our skills, look at our resources, and examine what was motivating us. We weighed the benefits and explored the consequences of not following through with our dream. Potential obstacles were identified along with possible solutions. Upon completion of our systematic goal-planning process, we developed a comprehensive business plan.

Some of our friends and colleagues thought a married couple working together was a recipe for divorce. We knew we had the recipe for our success. And we were right. Right, Charles?

Charles

That's right, Annarose. It is the same message we bring to our clients. There is no "silver bullet." If there is something you want to achieve, you have to take action to make it happen. In our case, we wanted to be successful working together. And by planning, goal-setting, and persistence we made it happen.

Wright

How does your personal relationship affect how you do business?

Annarose

David, you said the magic word—"relationship." It's all about relationships. Our personal relationship provides the basis for our business relationship, which in turn is how we relate to our clients. I guess you might say we are in the relationship business.

Our personal relationship is founded on respect. Charles and I hold each other in high regard. We accept each other for who we are and what we have to offer. At the same time we recognize we are individuals with different personalities, skills, and reference points. We understand that we are influenced by our different backgrounds and experiences. Yet by respecting our differences, Charles and I strengthen our relationship and enrich our lives both personally and professionally.

And believe me David, Charles and I are very, very different. Obviously we are of opposite genders and you may have noticed from our conversation, I tend to be the more outgoing and talkative partner. Charles prefers to consider himself "reserved."

In the professional arena, Charles has led corporations that employed hundreds of people. My background has been more eclectic and focused on working with others on an individual basis.

Our upbringings are also contrasting. I was raised in a nontraditional family, in a big house, in a small town; Charles was raised in a traditional family, in a small apartment, in a big city. We also come from diverse religious cultures. My Christian background is quite different from Charles' Jewish background. Yet from the beginning, Charles and I embraced our differences and interfaith relationship with enthusiasm, understanding, and a willingness to share in each other's practices.

Respect for each other, regardless of differences, is what we bring from our personal relationship to each client relationship. Early on we learned to capitalize on our diversity and maximize our similarities. And we know we have many more similarities than differences. We share common values and interests, a love for our family and, unfortunately, very high golf scores.

Charles

Let's forget about the golf scores☺. As Annarose said, for a relationship to be successful it is vital the individuals respect each other and accept each other for who they are. With respect comes a valuing of different perspectives. And by capitalizing on the differing perspectives, new and exciting opportunities are created.

I know it sounds like such a simple formula. Unfortunately, we have noticed that the culture of some organizations fosters a neglect of the "respect factor." The impact of lack of respect and acceptance of diverse opinions in the workplace manifests itself in many ways. For example, we have witnessed destructive gossip, we've seen co-workers deliberately withhold information or assistance from each other, and we've heard such phrases as, "that's not how we do things around here," when a new idea is proposed. The list goes on and on.

It is this lack of respect for each other that can result in the breakdown of relationships. And when relationships break down, often a breakdown of morale is right behind it. With decreased morale comes decreased productivity. Decreased productivity translates to decreased profits.

The principle of respect and capitalizing on each other's differences builds successful relationships. And we know that successful businesses are built on successful relationships.

Wright

Besides respecting and capitalizing on each other's differences, are there other practices you bring from your personal relationship that apply to successful business strategies?

Annarose

Good question, David. We incorporate many other practices from our personal relationship into our business strategy. We also encourage our clients to adopt similar practices to enhance their business strategies. Keeping up with new and innovative trends is vital for a business. It is just as important, and perhaps even more important, to not lose sight of the fundamental practices that sustain success.

Let's look at three fundamental practices: sharing a common goal, communicating effectively, and maintaining a sense of humor.

In both our personal and professional lives, Charles and I are a team. We see ourselves as a team. And we know that among many other guiding principles, in order for our team to be successful, we need to build it around a shared goal. Our common goal is to live a healthy and prosperous life together.

By keeping our goal front and center, Charles and I trust that each will do what has to be done to achieve that goal, whether it involves eating a well balanced meal, working odd hours to fulfill a commitment, or assisting a client to uncover breakthrough opportunities. Sharing a common goal not only gives us a target to aim for but also provides us with purpose.

So even though each day we might be performing a variety of individual tasks, when necessary we evaluate problems together, develop strategies, and make decisions on various aspects pertaining to our life together. We are well aware that we can achieve more and deliver far more together than we can as individuals.

Similarly, as many of our clients move to adopt teamwork as an effective way to manage their organizations, we encourage them to look to their mission statement to identify their common goal. The mission statement tells everyone, from the CEO on down the organizational chart, the one reason they were hired. A fiscal employee and a field employee may have varied job responsibilities and rarely interact, yet both were hired for the same reason—to fulfill the organization's mission and common goal.

Charles

Often we find employees lose sight of why they were hired and/or never knew the reason from the start. They have no concept of their purpose and their importance to the organization. Without such focus, successful teaming is almost impossible. Too often Annarose and I see the "silo" mentality emerge where one department is pitted against another. This can create an adversarial work environment which can prove to be detrimental to the morale, health, and success of the organization.

Knowing the goal and one's role in contributing to the goal adds to the collective success of the team and increases one's sense of belonging and self-worth. It's a pretty safe bet that morale will increase along with productivity and ultimately the organization's bottom line.

Annarose

Communicating effectively is another practice Charles and I bring from our personal relationship that is fundamental to a successful business strategy. A few years ago I read an article written by Brian Tracy about the importance of effective communication skills in advancing one's career and personal life. In the time we have been together, Charles and I have been working diligently to develop this critical skill. It takes practice and persistence to become an effective communicator.

Communication seems so easy. We learn to talk at a very young age. In our case, Charles and I both speak English. I say something and he should understand what I am saying. Unfortunately it doesn't always work that way. Each of us has filters that can create barriers that can break down the communication process. Filters include our habits, culture, knowledge, age, gender, etc.

When I speak with Charles, or anyone, I have to remember to respect the filters and recognize the barriers so I can successfully get my message sent and understood in the same way it was intended.

Let me give you an example how the "good old gender" filter can create a barrier to effective communication. Many years ago, early in our relationship, Charles asked me what I wanted to do Saturday afternoon. I quickly answered, "Well we could go to a movie, but it is too nice outside. I don't want to go inside. Or we could go shopping, but I don't like to go shopping on the weekends—it is too crowded. Or maybe we could take a hike down by the river, but . . ." When I was half-way through the third item out of my verbal suggestion box, I noticed Charles' eyes had glazed over.

It was at that moment I felt a power surge come over me and I realized I had lost the poor man—too many words! He was confused. He asked a simple, straight-forward question and I shared with him a litany of alternatives and dumped all my thoughts, as I usually do with my girlfriends. I simply wasn't speaking "his" language. I needed to speak the language he could understand. So I gave him a direct answer, "Let's hang out on the back porch and play cards." To which he responded, "Great." End of conversation.

In order to be an effective communicator we have to be willing to adapt our style of communication to fit the other person's style. After all, when we travel to a different country where people are culturally trained to speak a different language, don't we make an effort to communicate in their language?

Charles and I come from separate gender cultures, so it is no surprise we have very distinct communication styles. As male and female, we have been culturally trained to communicate differently and it is our individual responsibility to be flexible. Since women comprise almost 50 percent of today's workforce, both genders must be knowledgeable and sensitive to the other gender's communication style. Keep in mind, effective communication builds relationships and relationships build business.

Charles

David, when we facilitate communication skills training and introduce the inter-gender segment, participants are fascinated to learn of the inherent cultural communication gaps between the genders. We can feel the excitement in the room as they realize that a few minor adjustments to how they communicate with the opposite gender just might save a relationship—on or off the job.

Annarose

That's right Charles, how we speak to each other is important, and how we listen is equally important. Listening promotes understanding. And don't we all want to be understood?

I consider Charles to be a good listener. He doesn't interrupt me, try to finish my sentences, or become distracted when I speak to him. Charles exhibits good listening habits.

Charles

What—are you talking to *me* Annarose?

Annarose

Give me a break! Charles, you and I both know that hearing and listening are not synonymous. The value of listening is often overlooked but it is vital for effective communication. People tend to gravitate toward people who listen. Right, Charles?

Charles

Yes, Annarose. And people tend to do business with businesses that listen.

Annarose

Listening requires an intentional effort. In grade school I was taught, as you probably were as well, how to read, how to spell, and even how to solve math problems. Unfortunately, I was never taught *how* to listen. The teachers would say, "Don't you understand? Aren't you listening?" To tell the truth, I thought I was listening. I wish I knew then what I know now—listening is an active process and a skill that can be learned.

Now, I practice the skill of active listening. I have an attitude of "wanting to listen." I ask questions for clarification; I use other techniques such as paraphrasing and perception checking; I watch body language; and I demonstrate empathy. This concentrated effort helps me to hear, interpret, and evaluate what is being said and how it is being said. It increases my understanding of the message so I can respond appropriately.

Today's work environment is often defined by stress and constant change which can lead to misunderstandings, redundancy, and errors. Active listening promotes understanding, efficiency, and clarity.

Charles

That's true. Active listening is also essential for a relationship to be successful. It is our first step in establishing a trusted partnership with each client. Being able to understand our clients' concerns enables us to approach each engagement as a unique project. Active listening makes good business sense.

Annarose

Lastly, and perhaps the most versatile practice from our personal relationship that applies to successful business strategies, is maintaining a sense of humor. Just as many couples have had their ups and downs, so too have Charles and I. The value of being able to laugh at ourselves has always helped us through the trying times and added to the good times.

Whenever we are facilitating a training program or presenting a keynote address we make sure participants have the opportunity to laugh. Laughter adds to the learning environment. It is my philosophy that if participants are laughing, they are listening, and if they are listening it increases the chances they are learning. And besides, my mom always says, "Laughing is good for you."

Sometimes participants tell us about adversarial and stressful work situations. They say there is little room for good-natured humor and they rarely laugh while on the job. On the other hand, we have seen corporate cultures where healthy humor is embraced. Humor can diffuse conflict, ignite creativity, relieve stress, and create bonds that enhance relationships.

Wright

We have been talking about how relationships impact business strategies. What are your thoughts Charles?

Charles

Glad you asked, David. If you let Annarose continue, she'll not only disclose all of her thoughts, she will also tell you some of mine.

Annarose

Very funny, Charles.

Charles

David, at the very beginning of our business partnership, Annarose was stressing the word "relationships." She kept saying, "It's all about relationships." I have to admit, as a seasoned CEO, I cringed when I thought of marketing the concept of "relationships" to other executives. It just sounded too soft.

When thinking about "relationships" I was focused on interpersonal relationships—albeit a very important aspect—but not how I wanted to differentiate our marketing strategy. After further analysis, both the soft and hard aspects of the "relationship concept" become apparent. I realized, in addition to the conventional person-to-person relationship, there is also the person-to-process relationship, and the process-to-process relationship.

Annarose

Charles became enlightened.

Charles

Yes, you can say that.

For almost a decade, Annarose and I have been working with organizations to help build effective workforce, workplace, and systems relationships. One way we do this is through the development and implementation of a well-designed performance management system.

Performance management is both a process and a system. The process encourages team members to perform to the best of their abilities while the system is positive, performance-based, and ongoing. Performance management provides employees with opportunity, guidance, and direction, along with built-in controls for the organization.

The goal of performance management is to:

- Enhance the employee-to-supervisor relationship by fostering communication, engaging employees, and supporting achievements.

- Strengthen the supervisor-to-process relationship by creating a user friendly tool to help supervisors objectively measure performance based on established competencies and company goals.
- Streamline the process-to-process relationship by creating a seamless mechanism that links the performance management process with other processes such as advancement, bonuses, and/or merit pay increases.

Let me give you a quick overview of our *Six-Step Performance Management System.*

Step 1—Establish Clear Expectations

This Step is an on-going process that begins when a newly hired employee's job duties, competencies, and expectations are defined. The employee is provided with the organization's mission and vision statements. The employee is made aware of the valuable role he or she plays in helping the organization achieve its goals. The process only ends when the employee leaves the organization.

Step 2—Maintain a Competency Inventory

Based on the Clear Expectations, each supervisor maintains a Competency Inventory for each assigned employee. Competencies are the skills, values, and behaviors that are critical to success. The competencies are clearly defined, observable, and measurable. The Competency Inventory measures employee strengths and weaknesses and identifies any performance gaps.

Step 3—Write Goals

Based on the strengths and gaps identified in the Competency Inventory, the supervisor and employee work together to develop performance goals. It is also important for the supervisor and the employee to collaborate on growth goals that open channels of communication and create an engaged employee.

Step 4—Conduct Performance Check-Ins

Regular Performance Check-Ins encourage employee-supervisor dialogue and build healthy work relationships. Check-Ins create an opportunity for constructive feedback and discussion on progress toward goals.

Step 5—Maintain a Performance Log

The Performance Log enables the supervisor to track each employee's performances and any action, positive or negative, taken in response to the performance. The Performance Log serves as a memory jog throughout the process.

Step 6—Complete Formal Evaluation

The Formal Evaluation is based on the employee's performance as discussed during Performance Check-Ins and documented in the Performance Log. When conducted effectively there are no surprises for the employee. The Evaluation becomes an objective summary of the employee's performance. It is a meaningful resource for both the supervisor and the employee.

Annarose

At the conclusion of the Formal Evaluation, the process begins all over again. Keep in mind, for performance management to be effective, it is essential for supervisors to be well trained in how to use the tool, provide constructive feedback, and coach their employees.

Charles

Also, to leverage the performance management system the organization must take a team approach to its design and administration. Upper management needs to support and contribute to the effort.

We consult with the chief executive officer, human resource directors, and supervisors to ensure the performance management system is aligned with corporate goals and is viewed as a core component in the overall business strategy.

In short, effective performance management fosters better working relationships and builds successful businesses.

Wright

It sounds as if, in the ROI Training & Consulting firm, Annarose is the training component and Charles focuses on consulting. Am I correct?

Charles

Yes and no. There are times Annarose will design and facilitate a training program without me. And on occasion I will take a consulting assignment on my own. However, the majority of our work is conducted as a team.

Annarose

When providing one-on-one coaching, Charles and I usually divide along gender lines. I have a deep commitment to helping women in leadership—women new to leadership positions, and women transitioning back into the workforce tap into to their potential and achieve success.

The majority of Charles' coaching clients are experienced male executives.

Charles

With few exceptions, we share the training and consulting responsibilities. Our strength lies in our working together and capitalizing on our differences to create something much greater. Working as a team enables us to better fulfill our mission to help organizations and individuals identify, plan, and achieve professional and personal goals. Our clients seem to appreciate the contributions both of us make and the dual perspective we bring to the table.

Wright

Tell me a little more about this dual perspective you provide to your clients.

Annarose

As we have been saying throughout this interview, Charles and I work as a team. At the same time, we know we are individuals with different experiences, ideas, and ways of approaching solutions. We naturally see things from different perspectives.

Charles is goal-focused and always cognizant of business results. He looks at the overtly measurable components of a situation and then works backward. On the other hand, I am process-focused and more in tune with the elements of a situation. I work up to business results. Together we blend the two perspectives to create a relationship between the quantitative and qualitative components.

Charles

Here is an example of our dual perspective in action: A client engages us to design and facilitate a customer service training program. My thoughts immediately focus on how the client will achieve a measurable return on the organization's investment—how we will measure the impact of the training program on the company's bottom line. I am looking to answer such questions as, "How will we establish our baseline, compare results, and determine the operational impact? Specifically, what results do we want to achieve and how will we measure them?"

Annarose

Unlike Charles, I begin by determining what information the participants will need to increase their awareness, develop skills, and change their behavior. I look to answer, "How can we provide a meaningful learning experience that enables participants to transfer learning to performance?"

I look at the program through the eyes of the participant and focus on the relationship between the participant and the training.

Charles looks at the program through the eyes of the executive and focuses on the relationship between the organization and the training.

I determine learning results while Charles is fixed on business results.

Keep in mind, neither perspective is exclusive. When the program is completed, it will support employee development while addressing company-specific objectives.

Charles

This dual perspective is our strength. It is working through the differences that creates synergy and a stronger end product for our clients.

Wright

Charles and Annarose, you make blending personal and professional success sound so easy. Is it really that easy?

Charles

Thank you, David, that is a very nice compliment. Sometimes it is hard work to make something look easy. Doesn't Tiger Woods make golf look easy? Yet he is often the first on the course practicing his swing and reviewing his game plan.

Annarose

Charles and I are equally persistent, hard-working, and determined to achieve success. We take nothing for granted and appreciate the opportunities we are given.

Wright

Before we wrap up our talk, exactly what does ROI stand for?

Charles

Return on Investment.

Annarose

Results Oriented Instructors.

Charles

David, you have just witnessed our dual perspective first hand!

Wright

Annarose and Charles, it has been a pleasure speaking with both of you today about your success. We touched on many topics. You reminded us of the importance of focusing on fundamental practices to build successful personal, professional, and business relationships. I even learned a new word—"coprenuers."

Today we have been speaking with Annarose Ingarra-Milch and Charles Milch, owners of ROI Training & Consulting. They rely on their synergy to help their clients build relationships to achieve success.

About The Authors

COPRENUERS ANNAROSE INGARRA-MILCH AND CHARLES MILCH own ROI Training & Consulting. They are nationally recognized speakers, facilitators, coaches, and management consultants.

Their clients include the Department of the Navy, the Pennsylvania Chamber of Commerce Executives Association (PCCE), the Pennsylvania Association of Nonprofit Organizations (PANO), and the Pennsylvania State American Association of University Women (AAUW).

ROI also provides services to other industry sectors including educational institutions, financial institutions, manufacturing companies, trade associations, service providers, and nonprofit organizations.

Annarose and Charles share a passion for developing the leaders of tomorrow by teaching college courses. Both volunteer their time and serve on the boards of directors of statewide and community-based nonprofit organizations.

The team of Annarose and Charles know the value of relationships. They tap their synergetic relationship and natural dual perspective to challenge businesses to maximize their workforce, workplace, and systems relationships to achieve success.

Annarose Ingarra-Milch and Charles Milch
ROI Training & Consulting
1855 Alsace Road
Reading, PA 19604
Phone: 610.378.9499
E-mail: roi-aim@msn.com
www.theconsultantsforum.com/roi.htm

Chapter 4

ARTHURETTA MARTIN

THE INTERVIEW

David Wright (Wright)

Today we're talking with Arthuretta Martin. She is a wife and mother, student, motivational speaker, small business advocate, parents' rights advocate, civil rights advocate, trainer, vocalist, civil servant, actress, and published author.

Arthuretta, welcome to *Speaking of Success.*

Arthuretta Martin (Martin)

It is good to be here. I'm excited about the opportunity to be a part of this project.

Wright

We are here today to talk about success. We all want to be successful but it means many things to many people. First let me ask you, what does success mean to you? Secondly, of all the things you've done and accomplished in your life, what do you feel the most successful in having achieved?

Martin

I guess that is a good place to start. Success has a different meaning for me today than it had in the earlier part of my life. During the first half of my life I went for what I wanted. I was goal focused and continuously and persistently pursued those goals. I pursued my goals and even though some of my choices were not the best, I succeeded.

I thought I was in love and like most teenagers, I didn't like to listen to my parents because they didn't know anything—or so I thought. I was married at eighteen, a mother of two by twenty-one, and divorced by twenty-four. I was then faced with reality: I only had a high school education and no marketable skills. I moved back home with my parents, enrolled in college, and got a part-time job with the federal government. In three years I finished college with a bachelor's degree in public administration. Achieving that degree despite the odds is something that I've been proud to achieve.

My degree was only a ticket to board the train for professional success though. Getting on the train was another struggle. I had to obtain a professional position. The cycle of struggle, tenacity, persistence, and achievement began. Since that time I've been promoted ten times, achieving the title of Deputy Director of the Office of Small and Disadvantaged Business Utilization at the Department of Health and Human Services, I've obtained a master's degree in management, taken course work toward a PhD, remarried, and had one more child. I guess you could say I look like a success.

Wright

You "look like a success?" That is an interesting way to say that you don't see yourself as a success although others may. Don't you see yourself as successful?

Martin

Yes and no. I am an exception to what happens to teenagers who get pregnant. From that perspective I am definitely a success because I've overcome challenges and obstacles to improve the quality of my life and those of my family. Yet I know there is more to what I can contribute than where I am today. My experiences in life—especially working for the government—have caused me to re-evaluate what I define as successful. Accomplishing a goal is a form of success, yet if the goal established does not add to your purpose in life is it a success?

Wright

I had not thought of success as different from accomplishing purpose. Tell me more.

Martin

I believe that each person born arrives on earth with a specific purpose. In the United States our living conditions are ripe for us to achieve purpose. Let me say this another way: success is something you achieve for yourself—purpose is something you achieve that improves the quality of life for generations to come. Accomplishing your purpose—not simply successfully completing goals—contributes to the benefit of all humankind. We are each given a host of gifts by God to accomplish that purpose. I believe we can accomplish a series of goals in our lives. Some of those goals contribute to our purpose. Some of them are simply a goal achieved. And some of our goals achieved actually derail us from purpose (like getting married at eighteen years old). Success in life should be measured by how accomplishing our goals supports our purpose.

Wright

Can you give me an example?

Martin

Sure. If my purpose and my gifts are to teach children to read and write and I only perform jobs in a factory making widgets, then regardless of how many widgets I produce in a day, I am not living a successful life.

A biblical example is Jonah. Jonah successfully ran from his purpose for years. He accomplished his goal of sneaking onto a fishing ship. Running from his purpose—despite his success—was not accomplishing purpose. Sneaking onto the ship helped him to accomplish a purpose even though he didn't realize it at the time. He had a goal of avoiding his call—his purpose—and for a while he succeeded. I'm sure Jonah saw his time in the belly of the big fish as a failure. But it was at that time he began to live his purpose.

It is interesting that in life, today's apparent success can be tomorrow's failure and vise versa. What appears to be a failure or a bad experience today can be a blessing in disguise. Jonah's experience in the big fish was certainly unpleasant. Yet he matured during those three days. That time perfected him. He succeeded in accepting his purpose and most importantly he accomplished his purpose by speaking to the people of Ninevah. He encouraged them to change from their evil behavior and turn to God. Jonah accomplished purpose in spite of himself.

Wright

I don't think most people see success in that way.

Martin

I know. Far too many people live their entire lives not living in purpose or even knowing they have one. I was one of those people. Most people are searching for something. That something—that yearning inside that we all have—is the search not only for purpose but also for the fulfillment of that purpose. But too often I believe they confuse success with accomplishing purpose.

You know the age-old question: why am I here? In our search to find purpose some people make many changes in their lives. Some people make dramatic career changes because they realize that their success in accomplishing goals did not help them to be fulfilled.

You've heard the stories of the lawyers turning to farming or the accountants who become florists. Seldom do we know our purpose from the beginning. We spend countless years searching. The blessed persons are those who find their purpose. Grandma Moses comes to mind. Her purpose was not defined until she was over ninety years old! This is why I like the phrase Tavis Smiley coined and used as the title of his book, *Never Mind Success . . . Go for Greatness.* I would like to add that success is not great until it leaves a deposit on the earth for the next generation.

Wright

Now that you mention it I can think of many people who experienced many failures until they achieved the success that resulted in greatness. Men like Walt Disney, J. C. Penny, John Wesley, and Thomas Edison are just three that come quickly to mind. These men had mediocre success until they slipped into purpose and built huge financial empires—greatness in deed.

Martin

Yes, and there are countless others whose measure of greatness was not financial but included contributions to the improvement of humanity. I am sure that Mother Theresa, Gandhi, and Dr. Martin Luther King lived their purpose. This measure of success is tough because they achieved greatness through pain, sacrifice, and death. Dr. King wanted Africans in America to be treated fairly, he saw his purpose as an instrument of that vision. He was willing to sacrifice his life and the well being of his family for that vision—and he did. In corporate America's standards he would not be seen as a success because we primarily measure success in dollars and cents. Marcus Garvey believed that Africans in America would never be treated fairly and advocated for disassociation from the United States and returning to Africa. Although the movement he envisioned was never fulfilled, his ideology continues to be studied and respected to this day.

I am sure that people did not see Nelson Mandela as a success during his twentieth year in a South African prison. As a matter of fact, the South African government saw their efforts as successful because they "controlled" the leader and kept him from achieving freedoms for his people. Yet by the twenty-fifth year, Mr. Mandela's faith and tenacity helped him to accomplish one of the greatest success stories in modern history. Mr. Mandela's suffering and apparent failures were the foundation for greatness and accomplishment of purpose—bringing an end to apartheid. Mr. Mandela "lived in the belly of the fish" for twenty-five years. But when it was time and he had been perfected, he accomplished marvelous and miraculous feats. John Brown was hung to death at Harper's Ferry yet his contributions to the liberation of Africans in America left an everlasting contribution to the improvement of the human race for generations to come. If we were to measure John Brown's life from economic standards he was an utter disgrace—a failure. Yet he accomplished his purpose.

And oh yes, I can't forget the contribution of Harriet Tubman to my quality of life. She was a success when she escaped from slavery. She fulfilled purpose when she went back and saved ninety-two others. Each of these individuals was seen as a threat to oppressive power structures. Some lost their natural lives to live eternal lives because they were willing to make the ultimate sacrifice and fulfill their purpose.

Wright

Tell me how do you personally relate to these stories?

Martin

I see myself in the belly of the big fish right now. I wanted to be a civil servant. I wanted to continue the legacy of Dr. King and the countless Africans in America before me who had a dream that our people would have the same rights and privileges of every other American. I wanted to contribute and build upon that legacy through public service and make a comfortable living at the same time.

The reality is that the government is made up of people with competing agendas. Most want to be successful. To accomplish that goal, many civil servants must compromise the greater good for professional success. Today the federal government's focus appears to be more toward protecting the interests of the "haves" as opposed to the "have nots." The culture is that bigger is better—the haves are to have more and the have nots are to have less.

While I originally thought that my professional success could be intertwined in continuing the legacy of my forefathers and mothers, I now see that the two are not compatible. In order to be successful today as a federal civil servant one must be willing and able to protect the interests of those with power. As I have moved up in my career I've found myself in a constant battle in making decisions and taking actions based on my conscience and the desires of my employer. This has been a very uncomfortable and extremely stressful place to be.

Like many of my fellow civil servants, once I realized the realities of civil service, I decided to go along as best I could to get along. I was going to hide out in the government, pull a secure salary, and retire at a ripe young age. Well, I believe that God is moving me out of my comfort zone to a place where He will be able to use me so that I can accomplish my purpose.

Notwithstanding my experiences I still have a purpose. Notwithstanding other people's experiences they still have purpose. I am at peace with knowing that I will achieve that purpose despite how things look today. My purpose involves improving the quality of life for those less fortunate. I believe it also involves helping people to realize that they do not have to compromise their integrity and self-worth to make a living. Their life can be worthwhile. Events occur that confirm this understanding for me. An opportunity like participating in this book project comes along and I am provided the opportunity to share this message. I'm being perfected for a work to make a contribution to improve the human condition.

Wright

That is a mighty big statement. Success versus purpose is certainly a different way to look at life accomplishments.

Martin

Yes, success versus purpose is different. I believe people like Oprah Winfrey are very successful but neither their financial success nor their fame was their purpose. Oprah's purpose is giving to the less fortunate, helping people heal emotionally, and being an example for women like me who struggle with their weight. If Oprah can lose weight, so can I!

Denzel Washington is another example. Denzel is seen as someone who is a man's man. An accomplished actor, he is only the second African American to receive an Oscar for Best Actor. This is quite an accomplishment and a true measure of his success. However, I see purpose in his work as a director. His quiet strength as a father, husband, and leader in the community is his purpose. He is giving back. His recent movies bring attention to issues affecting the public. Movies like *Glory, Philadelphia, John Q,* and *Malcolm X* are just a few of his movies that give a voice to the voiceless.

Then there are the unsung heroes. My voice teacher, Anne Hurley Cole, is one of those people who live in purpose. Day after day she teaches people how to sing. Six to eight hours, seven days a week Anne works with and coaches each voice to be its best. She loves to teach. She may not have the notoriety of Oprah or the resources of Denzel but Anne is living in purpose. There are many teachers, nurses, doctors, police officers, artists, musicians, and astronauts who were born to do just what they are doing. They are living in purpose. But again, there are many teachers, nurses, doctors, police officers, artists, musicians, and astronauts who may be successful but their success may only be a stepping-stone for them to accomplish their purpose.

Former President Jimmy Carter successfully became President of the United States. However, I don't believe he began to live in his purpose until after his presidency and he was able to serve the poor and the disenfranchised world-wide.

Wright

Hmm . . . sounds like you are saying we should all live a "Purpose Driven Life." I believe I've read that somewhere before. You know, to do so can require you to sacrifice a great deal too.

In our preparation for your interview we noticed that you have authored several articles on federal employment. One in particular has caught my attention. You wrote an article and exposed how individuals who receive monetary settlements and judgments in employment discrimination cases are double taxed by the Internal Revenue Service. Will you share a bit more with our readers about this situation?

Martin

Yes I can. In 1996, Congress practically repealed the "make whole" provisions of the Civil Rights Act of 1964 by passing a little known rider to what was called the Small Business Protection Act.

That rider changed the way compensatory damages relating specifically to claims of discrimination and retaliation would be taxed. For the first time since the passage of the 1964 Civil Rights Act, emotional distress damages would be taxed, as well as back pay and front pay in the year that the damages were suffered. To add insult to injury, as a result of several Supreme Court decisions, attorneys' fees are also taxed, and payments awarded as a result of the claims cannot be income-averaged.

The result has been that, in many cases, not only is the individual not made whole, but he or she may actually owe the IRS thousands of dollars if he or she wins a discrimination lawsuit. If you are compensated for the humiliation you experience from a bar room brawl, you don't have to pay the federal tax; you are only required to pay it when you have prevailed in an employment discrimination case. Why would Congress do such a thing? Why would any President sign it into law?

Justice and restitution have truly suffered terrible blows. And for those of us who are the victims of employment discrimination the reality of the bittersweet victory is overwhelming. Our lives may go from broken to shattered after prevailing in a civil rights case.

For example, consider the case of Monica McFadden. After twenty years of being subjected to humiliating sexual harassment by the Chicago police force, Ms. McFadden won her claim of discrimination. She was awarded $300,000 in damages and almost $1 million for lawyers' fees and costs. However, not only did she lose every penny of the award, she owed the IRS $99,000 in taxes!

Another example is the 2001 case of Cynthia Spina. Ms. Spina won a case where she was awarded the maximum $300,000 against the Forest Preserve District of Cook County. Her employer had berated, belittled, and isolated her because of her sex. Unfortunately, Ms. Spina was awarded $850,000 in attorney fees and $100,000 in court costs. Ms. Spina was taxed at the highest tax rate and, like Ms. McFadden, wound up owing the IRS thousands of dollars. Magistrate Judge Arlander Keys, who had reduced the original jury award of $3 million to the $300,000, said he was "not unsympathetic to plaintiff's plight. Plaintiff waged a courageous fight for what she believed was just, even though other female officers who felt similarly victimized lacked the fortitude to do so." But, as we have heard so many times before . . . the law is the law.

On August 22, 2006, in the case of Murphy vs. the IRS, the U.S. District Court for the District of Columbia ruled this law unconstitutional. I am proud to say that my work and those I've worked with contributed to the public's awareness of this injustice. I wrote many articles on this and other subjects relating to employment matters. I recently did a Google search and found that my work has been reprinted in several Human Resource and Diversity publications.

Unfortunately, not everyone appreciates my vocal position on employment and civil rights issues. However, I believe that I've contributed and will continue to contribute to the improvement of the overall condition of employment both in the public and private sector. Accomplishing purpose requires short-term and even long-term sacrifices for the good of the many. My ability to articulate complex issues in writing in easy-to-understand concepts continues to help the movement for workers rights. Writing, however, is but one of my gifts. God has blessed me with many gifts and talents. How they will be used to accomplish my purpose is an ever-evolving process and I am a yielding vessel.

Wright

Speaking of your gifts and talents, they are indeed many. You act, you do public speaking, you write, and you also sing, correct?

Martin

Yes I do. I sing several different types of music from gospel to classical. I am now pursuing a career as a jazz vocalist. I hope to release my first CD this year.

My acting is limited to small productions. However, I'm now being considered for motion pictures and theater opportunities. Like singing, it is a gift that I have not maximized. My prayer is to do more to edify the spirits of those who are hurting, those who are frustrated, and those who need encouragement. I have a lot of work to do during the second half of my life. You are never too old to begin again!

My published writing is primarily as an activist and advocate for federal employee due process rights. I realized early in my career that if federal employees lacked due process rights, they would not be able to protect due process rights of the American public. This is a perfect example of being successful and not fully understanding the consequences of that success.

A partner and I did a good year of research on this subject. We identified the weaknesses in the laws and regulations and published our findings with the hope of encouraging Congress and employee groups to advocate and strengthen the law. The result was predictable for anyone inside Washington politics—we were not successful. Members of Congress largely ignored our findings, and federal agencies filled the holes in the laws without strengthening federal employees' due process rights. As a matter of fact, due process rights have severely eroded over the past ten years. Employee organizations and labor lawyers could not refute the findings so they ignored the findings and ostracized us. For many reasons people want the system to remain unchanged.

But the wind of change is shifting and the public is increasingly aware that our government must continue to protect workers' rights. Through these experiences I learned how critical relationships are to politics and that success is measured not just by what you accomplish but also by the impact of your efforts. For what it is worth, the Equal Employment Opportunity Commission has clarified its due process procedures for federal employees. Although we will not get credit for this change, as was the case with our work on the double taxation issue, I know we were successful in bringing the matter to the public's and Congress's attention.

Wright

I now see how you describe yourself as an advocate and activist. I also understand why you believe your success is intertwined with accomplishing your purpose.

Martin

Yes, and civil rights is not the only area I have advocated. I've advocated for the rights of disabled children, ethical medical care for both the insured and uninsured, and business opportunities for small businesses. If I am not advocating, it doesn't matter to me how much money I make or how big my house is or even how important my job title may be, I will not see myself as successful.

Wright

Do you believe your musical talents and drive to accomplish purpose can evolve together?

Martin

Yes, I do. People like Maya Angelo did it, Paul Robeson did it, and even Marian Anderson did it. And if you listen closely to some of the music of today, words of advocacy are intertwined throughout. The arts have always been a tool for advocacy in the African American community.

Wright

Tell me, why do you believe you did not pursue a musical career in the earlier part of your life?

Martin

I am a classical singer. Believe it or not, classical music was not embraced in my community. I didn't have role models to help nurture my musical gifts. However, there were many civil rights advocates in my community. Continuing the legacy of protecting civil and human rights became my goal. I was not exposed to role models who were both activists and artists. As a matter of fact, history books in the American education system are silent on the artistic contributions of people like Paul Robeson, Harry Belafonte, James Baldwin, and Nikki Giovani to the Civil Rights Movement. I didn't even hear about the courageous stand taken by opera singer Marian Anderson until I was an adult. Perhaps if I had known about that I would have continued the legacy of such giants in the Movement—my artistic abilities would not have lain dormant for so long. It is important for the gifts children possess to be nurtured and for them to be directed to use those gifts to live their purpose. But that is another topic for another time.

Wright

I sense courage in your character. No doubt you have already contributed to the lives of many and have left a lasting mark. Are there any words of advice you want to leave with our readers?

Martin

Yes, I have seven:

1. Spend a lot of time with God through study and meditation and then yourself—get to know yourself through the eyes of God first. That is the only way you will learn your purpose. Once you believe you've found your purpose, put everything you have into accomplishing it. Only then will you be able to establish goals and succeed at the goals that lead you to accomplish your purpose. Pray without ceasing.
2. Do your best in each task you undertake. By doing so you will leave each situation better than the way you found it. Pray without ceasing.
3. Even though it is sometimes difficult, try and find the good in all people. You may say or do something that could encourage a cold heart to melt. And when you can't find anything good, keep your mouth shut about it. Prayer will give you the strength to accomplish even this.
4. Never ever compromise your integrity for a dollar bill. I was once told my conscience was overactive. History has shown it is better for a conscience to be overactive than under-active, or not active at all. Success is not only measured by how much money you make, how big a home you have, how many parties you are invited to, or how many letters come before or after your name. Succeeding at accomplishing material wealth alone can cause you to succeed at losing your soul. Pray without ceasing.
5. Greatness, accomplishing purpose, prosperity, and success are not all the same. They are independent. Through prayer and God's direction you will gain the wisdom to know the difference.

6. Do not be afraid to suffer. All great social movements were the result of the masses overcoming oppression from pain and misery. Suffering builds patience and patience builds character. With character you can accomplish great things. Without character you are subject to be easily managed. The peace of God through prayer will sustain you through the trials.
7. Stand up for your principles even if you stand alone. Your ability to do this one task will determine if you can have what it takes to obtain greatness—stand out from the crowd. With God you can accomplish great things.

Wright

Arthuretta, it was certainly a pleasure to include you in *Speaking of Success.* Your insight and wisdom have given me a new perspective of success. I look forward to great things from you. I'm glad to have met you.

Martin

Eyes have not seen nor have ears heard what will be created when people learn to live successful purposeful lives.

Thank you again for this opportunity to share.

About the Author

ARTHURETTA MARTIN currently holds the title of Deputy Director for the Office of Small and Disadvantaged Business Utilization at the Department of Health and Human Services. In that position she is responsible for advocating for the inclusion of small and minority owned businesses to obtain a fair share of the seven billion dollar procurement budget of the Department. Advocating for small business is not the only arena where Ms. Martin strives to protect the rights of American citizens—she has also held leadership positions in several nonprofit organizations including Blacks in Government, American Society of Public Administrators, Conference of Minority Public Administrators, and the NAACP Federal Sector Task Force. She was formerly vice president and is the co-founder of Federal Employees Against Discrimination. She is Director of Missions at her local Church, Greater Little Zion Baptist Church in Fairfax County, Virginia. Ms. Martin believes that in order for the American public's rights to be protected, the rights of employees must be maintained. She has over twenty-five years of Federal Civil Service and she holds a master's degree in Management and an undergraduate degree in Public Administration.

As a vocalist she has sung before audiences throughout the country. She has a wide repertoire, from classical songs such as "Summertime" from the Broadway hit *Porgy and Bess* and "Và godendo" (Serse) by Handel in E Flat to jazz in the spirit of Sarah Vaughn, Ms. Martin's vocal talents are captivating. She has studied voice under the direction of Edward Jackson of the Duke Ellington School of the Arts, vocal instructor to opera star Denise Graves, the late Leroy Dorsey of Howard University, vocal instructor to pop singers Donny Hathaway and Roberta Flack. She currently studies classical voice under the exceptional direction of Anne Hurley of Fairfax County, Virginia. She also studies jazz voice at the Elliston Institute of Jazz Studies from Ronnie Wells, founder of the East Coast Jazz Festival. Ms. Martin is working on several projects including a jazz tour that will feature standard and original tunes. She will soon release her first solo CD of Negro Spirituals in the spring of 2007. The objective of this is to not only encourage the spirit of the listener through these timeless classics, but also to preserve, celebrate, and improve the public's awareness and understanding of the Negro Spirituals. This release will feature the work of Harry T. Burleigh, a forgotten giant of American music, in high voice.

Arthuretta Martin
Phone: 703.946.6852
Fax: 703.426.0180
P.O. Box 2564
Springfield, Virginia 22152
E-mail: arthuretta5@verizon.net
www.arthurettasings.com

Chapter 5

June Kranich

THE INTERVIEW

David Wright (Wright)

Today we're talking with June Kranich. She began her successful sales career by working in the Vacation Ownership industry for a company with a hundred million dollars in annual revenues. After only one year in the field, June was promoted into training.

She then became Lead Trainer after two years, instructing between two hundred and three hundred sales representatives at any given time. Altogether June trained more than thirty-five hundred people and achieved a significant return on investment (ROI). As a result she was promoted to the position of general manager of the Training and Recruiting Department. She also has built a successful business in direct sales and is at the top of that company as well. While training, June developed her concept of "The Why Factor" to help people understand the internal motivators they need to succeed.

June, welcome to *Speaking of Success.*

June Kranich

Thank you for inviting me.

Wright

So how did you come up with the idea of "The Why Factor"?

Kranich

I came up with "The Why Factor" because I was training sales reps and in the training program we were talking a lot about "how"—how to overcome objections and how to close a sale. What I found was that the representatives were getting a little robotic because they knew "how" but they didn't have a clear and identified "why."

When they identified "why" they must succeed, the "how" was just a natural thing that followed.

Wright

Is this something you discovered as a result of experience in your own career?

Kranich

Yes it is. I had come to a crossroads in my own life. I started singing professionally, traveling extensively at the ripe old age of seventeen, and before I knew it, I had gotten caught up in the lifestyle that was so prevalent in the '80s. I was drinking and partying heavily and eventually my life spiraled out of control; I found myself in a place I didn't even know existed. By the age of twenty-nine, I was helpless, jobless, homeless, and defeated. It was then I knew I had two choices: One was to give in to the monkey on my back and continue to exist the best I could, hoping just to live long enough to see thirty. Or two, step up and step out of that bondage and that lifestyle and be the person God intended me to be.

That is where my journey began. I started from absolutely *nothing!* No direction, no purpose, and no passion. As a result of putting one foot in front of another, of believing that the impossible is possible, of tapping into all of the resources I could possibly find, I began a whole new life. There is at least one positive thing to being defeated and having nothing—you can go in whatever direction you choose.

Once I figured out that waitressing was not my calling and was not going to help me to fulfill my dreams, I looked into the magical world of sales. That is where my whole world really opened up! I had gotten a real estate license to sell residential real estate, but when I found out I needed about six months in savings, that was not going to be a reality for me—I was still broke.

I was introduced to the Vacation Ownership industry, which required a real estate license to earn commissions, and the rest is history as they say. I will never forget my first day of training, for it made a profound change in my life. The vice president of sales, Curt Knipe, said, "It doesn't matter what you've done up to this point in your life, what matters is what you are willing to do from today on. If you have a dream, a real estate license, and you are willing to work hard, then you are in the right place!" I knew that day that God had spoken to me and I had found what I was looking for—a chance.

Wright

Would you tell us what drives you toward success?

Kranich

I think that getting to such a low point in my own life was integral to my desire and my quest for success. When you come to such a low point in your life—a place you never ever expected to be—it can then propel you toward success that much more.

I also think there are two reasons: one, to make up for lost time and two, to prove to myself that I am much more than I have demonstrated. Now I'm on the other end of the spectrum. It has been almost a blessing; it was a cleansing period and it was a good thing for me to have had that experience. I view that failure as absolutely essential to my success. I always say, "Let your pain be a motivator and not a jailor." Those are principles that I live by.

Wright

What is it about success and self-improvement that you are so passionate about?

Kranich

Besides the obvious by-product, which is financial security and less stress, I think that what makes me so passionate about it truly is the human spirit and what we're all capable of.

Everybody's idea of success is different and I am not necessarily talking just about financial gain. All of us have this God-given desire for success placed inside of us naturally. But it gets clouded and covered up in many people by fear of failure, fear of rejection, fear of everything. We are such fear-ridden creatures that we literally lose the ability to even try anymore because the fear of failure far outweighs the triumph of success. So we settle for average—the status quo.

What I think is amazing is to see someone tap into their own potential and to see that person build upon it. That's what I love about success—to see others uncover it within themselves as well as within myself.

Wright

So in your case, was it all about change?

Kranich

Yes, absolutely. It was not changing one thing—it was changing *everything.*

Wright

So those were decisions that you made.

Kranich

Yes, and there are some key elements to change. The first one is what you just said—making a decision. It's just as simple as that. It's not anything more than just making that solid decision.

Secondly it's taking consistent, systematic, repetitive action. You don't go to a seminar once in a while where you get excited for a short time and then it fizzles away, just like you don't go to the gym one time and get in tip-top physical shape. It's consistency and persistence. It's viewing failure differently—looking at failure as the way to success. I read a great book titled *Failing Forward* by John C. Maxwell. It changed my view of failure. All my failures are what ultimately brought me to success—knowing that you *must* fail often to succeed once.

Self-development is another key element that we continually have to strive for. We have to go into the next level physically, spiritually, and mentally.

Lastly, it's believing that the impossible is possible. It is very important that you buy in to the fact that against all odds, it is possible.

Wright

Do you believe that there is a certain key element that *all* successful people have?

Kranich

I do, and I think that what makes people successful—what their common denominator is—is the way they think. The biggest thing I can think of is belief—unrelenting belief—that no matter what, you will think like a champion and conquer whatever you put your mind to.

Wright

Do you think there are common characteristics successful people have that others do not?

Kranich

Yes, I think that the most common characteristic is that successful people resist the urge to be average. Average is a very easy place to be. I once heard it said that average is the best of the worst and the worst of the best. Either way it is nothing to rave about. When you begin to succeed you will notice that people—your friends and those around you—treat you differently. When you raise the bar you remind them of their own failures and their own complacency. I think you have to always strive to go past that because average is acceptable, below average is not, and above average isn't either sometimes.

Wright

What do you think are some of the biggest obstacles people face in making long-lasting changes?

Kranich

I think the biggest obstacle is failure itself. We're such interesting creatures. As children, when we fell off a bike we would get back on repeatedly. If we asked for ice cream and Mom said, "No," we'd ask again five minutes later and if she still said, "No" we'd ask Dad. We just didn't let failure stand in our way. But as we grow and develop and we turn into adults who become fear based, and as we fail, we define ourselves by that failure. If you can let failure work for you instead of against you, I think that change in attitude can make a profound difference.

Wright

Why do you feel it is so very important to take the time to help others?

Kranich

Quite honestly, helping others will change who you are—it'll change your heart. When I say "help others" there are two different levels: There is the level of helping others and being compensated for it. And there's this whole other level called "volunteer." When you volunteer and you do it with no other agenda but to give back, I believe it changes who you are. I believe it will give you gratitude, understanding, humility, and compassion for others. I believe it is a spiritual law of life that we all must live by—the spiritual principle of giving—it is a very important part of my life and I wouldn't give it up for anything.

Wright

As you look back on your success and all the decisions you have made that led you to where you are today, has faith played an important role?

Kranich

Absolutely. There is a Divine Spirit and I think everybody knows that. Deep down inside of us, we all know this truth, and however you define your own spirituality is certainly a personal choice. You have to tap into that higher source that gives you strength when things look absolutely bleak. Faith means believing that things are going to work out no matter what. The thing about bad times is that there is always going to be a good time. When there's a high there's a low and vice versa. When there's rain, eventually there will be sunshine. It always balances itself out. I absolutely believe that faith is one of the biggest factors. Along with faith comes gratitude and we have to take a look around and be grateful for all that we have.

Wright

How does persistence play into the game of success?

Kranich

The dictionary definition of the word "persistence" is: refusing to relent, continuing in the face of opposition or interference. To me that says it all. It is easy to stay on course when everything is running smoothly, just as planned. However, continuing on in the face of opposition is what separates the good from the great. You see, to get above average results you must do above average things! Persistence is absolutely a key element to success. Without it, there would be no follow-through and therefore no payoff.

Wright

Someone told me once that if I saw a turtle on a fencepost that I could bet he didn't get up there by himself. Is there anyone in particular in your life who has played a role in developing who you are today?

Kranich

Yes there is and there are a couple of people who come to mind. The first person I can think of is my mother. My mother was an extremely persistent, strong-willed person with integrity and she believed there was nothing she could not do or that I could not do. When you're brought up around that kind of mentality I think it defines who you are.

Secondly, when entering the sales arena the vice president, Curt Knipe, was the person from day one who zeroed in on me. He said, "You are going to be great." He nurtured me for all those years and was my mentor. He believed in me before I believed in myself. To this day I'm grateful to him for seeing that in me.

This is what I think is so important about helping others. You can impact someone's life with your words—by showing that interest. At that time I needed to grab onto something and someone who believed in me because I couldn't see that in myself.

Wright

Where do you see yourself in the future? What kind of impact would you like to make and how do you want to be remembered?

Kranich

No matter what realm I'm in, I'm very passionate about helping others. I think many people are sitting in idle along the roadside of life waiting to hit the lottery! Instead, why not channel that energy toward yourself and making success happen? What gets me up in the morning is seeing other people tapping into their own potential because I know how it makes me feel.

I would like to be able to hear someone say that I helped them to see their own strengths and their own greatness as Curt did for me, for that is a blessing and a gift that no one can take away from me now. If I could just do that for a few people, that would be a great reward for me. That's why I am so passionate about speaking and writing—maybe, just maybe, something I say will impact someone along the way.

I want to be remembered as a person who absolutely refused to buy into the stereotypes, who believed that the impossible is possible, who wanted to help others, and who lived an extraordinary life—that is my prayer!

Wright

What a great conversation. I've enjoyed it and I appreciate your spending all this time with me answering all these questions. Your answers have been fascinating.

Today we have been talking with June Kranich who has been in the Vacation Ownership industry for quite some time and became General Manager of Training and Recruiting with a large company. She has also built a successful business in direct sales and is at the top of that company as well. She has trained thousands of people and has developed a new concept called "The Why Factor."

I think anyone who has read this chapter will get as much out of it as I have. I think she makes several very important points and I think she knows what she's talking about.

Thank you so much, June, for being with us today on *Speaking of Success.*

About the Author

JUNE KRANICH is a successful Speaker, Trainer, Consultant, and Coach with over ten years experience in sales and motivation. She specializes in sales particularly in the Vacation Ownership industry and has also managed to accomplish being at the top of her field in direct sales. Also, June brings the "Why Factor" into jails and institutions to help people find their true destiny in life. She is currently a member of the National Speakers Association.

June Kranich
June Kranich Enterprises
3248 Amberley Park Circle
Kissimmee, Fl. 34743
Phone: 407.929.0154
E-mail: ReachPotential@aol.com
www.JuneKranich.com

Chapter 6

DARLENE PRICE

THE INTERVIEW

David Wright (Wright)

Today we're talking with Darlene Price. Darlene is an internationally acclaimed executive speech coach, is the president of Well Said!, Inc., an organization dedicated to helping others speak and communicate more effectively. Chief officers and senior executives in the Fortune 100 and Global 2000 rely on Darlene for their speaking success, and she has trained over 5000 business professionals around the world. As the recipient of nine Telly Awards and one Emmy for outstanding corporate presentations, Darlene is a frequent expert source for the media, and conducts group workshops, private coaching, and keynote addresses. Darlene, welcome to *Speaking of Success.*

In your experience coaching chief officers and senior executives, what is the top indicator of a person's success in business today?

Darlene Price (Price)

I believe effective presentation and communication skills would have to be at the top of the list. I've conducted hundreds of interviews with the world's leading corporate executives and asked, "What is the number one skill you look for when hiring or promoting a candidate for senior management?" Over 90 percent say without hesitation that it is the ability to communicate effectively face-to-face, including the ability to stand and present ideas clearly and confidently to a group and relate well interpersonally one-on-one. Academic and industry studies reveal similar results. It's an exciting phenomenon to be a part of and I see it every day in the global business arena—the effective speakers and confident communicators get noticed, remembered, and promoted more quickly and more often than anyone else.

Wright

There are several core competencies that comprise a successful leader. Why do you think the majority of corporate executives seek face-to-face communication and presentation skills above the rest?

Price

Communication. As Plato observed, "Persuasion is the key to power," and effective face-to-face communication is the primary vehicle of influence. Through speech, powerful leaders clearly articulate their vision, communicate the value proposition for supporting the vision, and then ask for the votes to fund or produce the vision. I call it the 3V's of Leadership: Vision, Value, and Votes. The ability to communicate effectively face-to-face helps ensure success in all three areas.

A great example of this is my client, Grant. (Due to confidentiality agreements, I'll assign different names to my clients in the stories throughout our conversation). In the late '90s, Grant took over as president of a merger and acquisition nightmare. The company faced the worse employee and customer satisfaction scores in the industry due to repeated layoffs, years of insufficient research and development (R&D), and poor leadership, with former executives fired and charged for securities fraud and falsified accounting. Facing scandalous headlines, a falling stock price, and angry people, Grant took over. I reminded him of Winston Churchill's advice, "When you're going through hell, keep going." Indeed, Grant kept going guided by a primary mantra: Communicate. Communicate. Communicate. And communicate he did. In literally hundreds of meetings, Grant met with employees and customers face-to-face to communicate his vision for turning the company around. He confidently presented his plan of action and explained the benefits to everyone involved if they would join him in achieving the vision. Five years later he had clearly earned the votes.

Upon his retirement, the company boasted the best employee and customer satisfaction in the industry, an award-winning portfolio of products, and record-breaking sales and revenue growth. All of which contributed to a dramatic increase in the public valuation of the parent company. Trust was restored. Jobs were secure. People were happy.

Vision. An ancient proverb reads, "Where there is no vision, the people perish." Conversely, as Grant proved, where there is a compelling vision that is communicated clearly, the people prosper. It sounds obvious, but effective leaders lead. They take charge, set the course, guide the way, and pilot the people. Bottom line—they get results *through* people, not around them or despite them. That's good leadership, and good leadership requires good communication skills. As the saying goes, "If you think you're leading but no one is following, you're just taking a walk." Great leaders don't just take a walk. They inspire and motivate others to follow. And following requires feeling connected to the leader and his or her vision. Great leaders communicate with the primary purpose of connecting with their audience, whether it consists of employees, customers, prospects, the media, investors, Congress, or any key stakeholder because they know connection precedes commitment.

Value. Not only do great leaders verbally and vividly paint the vision of *what* we should be doing, they persuasively state the value proposition of *why* we should be doing it. Whether they're turning around a company, selling products and services, promoting operational excellence, managing change, or seeking budget approval, they present the payoff to the audience. They speak in terms of benefits and tell the audience what's in it for them to adopt the vision. Will it save lives? Improve the quality of life? Make us more money? Reduce risk? Lower costs? Improve efficiencies? Provide job security? Make the world a better place? For human beings, a change in movement usually requires a motive. "The fool persuades me with *his* reasons. The wise man persuades me with *my* own." Aristotle's words reveal the key to communicating value. Successful leaders take the time to know their audience—they communicate the value proposition from the perspective of their listeners, using *their* reasons.

Votes. Then, after clearly communicating vision and value, confident leaders ask for the vote. I've never worked with a chief officer or senior executive who was shy about asking for what they want. They expect their leaders to do the same. As Emerson said, "Speech is power: speech is to persuade, to convert, to compel." If you're presenting, then you're persuading at some level. The CEO of America's largest department store chain recently advised me on how to coach his executives. He said, "Tell them when they present to me to ask for what they need and why. I must know what they need from me to help drive their business." He wants his people to ask for his vote.

As we learned from Grant's story, when a leader knows how to clearly communicate a compelling vision and its resulting value to everyone involved, the people prosper. And producers of prosperity are highly sought after. I believe this helps explain why chief officers and senior executives seek and promote the face-to-face communication skill-set above the rest. Because there's always room at the top for more Grants—powerful communicators who can stand up in front of an audience of ten or ten thousand and who clearly present their vision and value will consequently earn votes that produce prosperity for the people.

Wright

Despite the desire to hire and promote successful speakers and communicators, isn't public speaking one of the top fears among people?

Price

Yes, in fact, according to *The Book of Lists*, the fear of public speaking ranks number one in the minds of the majority of people. Speaking in front of a crowd is above the fear of death, disease, snakes, and spiders. It's funny—we all want Andy Warhol's fifteen minutes of world-fame, but apparently we'd rather phone it in! The reasons are numerous and mainly fear-based: some of us fear failure, disapproval, embarrassment, and criticism; others fear the unknown, unanticipated questions, and forgetting. Then there's a version of perfectionism that can paralyze us and lead to unreal expectations, self-deprecation, and an all-or-nothing mindset. Finally, the person may simply lack the confidence, knowledge, and skill set to do a good job.

Any way you slice it, performance anxiety can be immobilizing. As a result, there isn't an overabundance of great speakers in the business world. Believe it or not, studies show only one in one hundred business people actually possess effective presentation skills at a proficient level. The good news is there's plenty of room for you and me to succeed! When you become a confident, dynamic speaker and presenter, you've not only mastered the most sought after skill in business today, you've also positioned yourself as a rare commodity, which increases your worth to the company and exposure to senior management.

My best advice is to learn to speak well, accept invitations to speak, and seek out opportunities to speak. We all feel some level of anxiety at the thought of addressing an audience. It takes courage to stand up and confidently present yourself and your ideas with passion and persuasion to a group of people. But it's worth it and pays double dividends when you do. The fear is real, but it pales in comparison to the success and advancement a person achieves when he or she learns to move through fear and speak up in spite of it. And let's not forget Emerson's comforting words, "Every great speaker was a bad speaker at first."

Wright

What advice can you offer to help us overcome stage fright and succeed at this crucial skill set?

Price

You can never get rid of the butterflies—you just teach them to fly in formation! And that's really the trick. Truth be told, you don't want to get rid of the butterflies because they're carriers of energy and enthusiasm. Adrenalin is your friend.

Years ago, one of the best speech coaches I ever trained with said to me, "Welcome the nerves, Darlene. They're a sign that you care and want to do a good job."

I replied, "Boy, I sure care a lot!"

The key is to control, harness, and focus that surge of adrenalin so that it works for you. To help with this, I created an acronym called STAGE MIGHT with my top ten favorite techniques:

1. *Smile.* Smile at yourself in the mirror before you speak, when you're introduced, and during your speech as appropriate. The physiological effect of smiling emits chemicals in the brain that calms the nerves and promotes relaxation. Plus a smile is the shortest distance between

two people. It shows your audience that you're happy to see them and enthusiastic about the message.

2. *Talk positively to yourself and visualize your success.* Let's learn from the experts in sports psychology. They've proven that an athlete's self-talk and visualizations create self-fulfilling prophecies—good or bad. Thoughts create action and actions create outcomes. Therefore, why not make them positive and reap the rewards? See in your mind your confident stride, warm smile, and adoring audience. And say to yourself, "I am a dynamic speaker." "I am enthusiastic and engaging." "I am liked by my audience." "I am prepared and confident." "I am on fire!" It really works.
3. *Acknowledge the three audience truths:* (1) They believe you're the expert. The audience perceives you as the recognized authority simply because you're the one speaking. Plus, you know more than they do about the topic. (2) They want you to succeed. The audience really wants you to be good and add value, otherwise it's a waste of their time. (3) They don't know what you're going to say. In the unlikely event you forget something or re-order your points, don't announce the error. They won't know.
4. *Greet and meet the audience before you speak.* Shake hands and talk with as many people as possible ahead of time. This shows the audience you're approachable and personable. Plus it relaxes you as the speaker and turns "public" speaking into "personal" speaking, which makes the presentation feel like a continued conversation.
5. *Exercise lightly backstage or privately before you speak to rid the body of excess adrenalin.* Do some light stretching, a few knee-bends, or take a brisk walk around the building. Plus take a few deep breaths. Inhale through the nose on a slow count of three and exhale through the mouth on a slow count of three.
6. *Memorize the first and last minutes of your presentation.* Knowing the first words that will come out of your mouth gives you confidence and calms your nerves. It also enables you to look directly into the eyes of your audience when you begin and optimize the first impression. Likewise, by nailing the closing, they'll remember you as confident and self-assured.

7. *Interact with your audience in the opening.* Within the first five minutes, involve the audience. Ask a thought-provoking question, conduct a survey by show of hands, ask audience members to introduce themselves (if appropriate), generate responses and make a list, do a learning activity, hold up a prop or give them a learning aid, tell a funny or compelling story. By immediately engaging your listeners, you focus the attention and interest where it belongs—on the audience—and not on you, which relieves some pressure. You're also doing something very natural and comfortable—interacting with human beings, rather than the feared "public speaking."
8. *Give, give, give.* Focus on giving to the audience. Often I'll ask people in my presentation workshops if they get overwhelmingly nervous when giving a birthday gift to a loved one. The answer is almost always no; rather, they feel anticipation, excitement, and joy. They look forward to it and eagerly await the unwrapping. As a speaker, think about your presentation as a present to the audience they will actually enjoy—a gift full of valuable information, helpful ideas, and meaningful content. The mental attitude of giving empowers you and frees you to focus on the purpose of the presentation—to inform and enrich the audience.
9. *Hold a dress rehearsal.* Comfort breeds confidence. The more you do it, the better you get. There's no better way to ensure a winning presentation or speech than to walk through it, say it aloud, practice your body movement, go through the slides, warm up your voice, and familiarize yourself with the content and flow. This way, when you stand up to speak, "it's not new, its déjà vu!" And ideally, videotape or audiotape the rehearsal and review your performance. Also, time the rehearsal to ensure you stay on schedule.
10. *Trust yourself.* There was a time when I was paralyzed by the fear that I would not have all the information I needed when making a presentation. One of my cherished coaches said to me, "Darlene, when you're making vegetable soup and you chop up ten carrots and place the pieces in the pot to simmer, do you worry the carrots will be missing when you return an hour later to serve it?" I answered, "Of

> course not." He said, "If you just relax and trust yourself, your content will be like the carrots. If you've prepared it, it'll be there for you when you lift the lid to serve—just believe in yourself." Trust yourself to be outstanding and you'll likely live up to your expectations.

And those are my tried and true tactics for turning stage fright into STAGE MIGHT. Hopefully these ten tips will help tame the butterflies and teach them to fly in formation!

Wright

What are the most common presentation pitfalls that stunt the success of business presenters and speakers?

Price

By far, it's the lack of rehearsal prior to the event. Before training a group, I send out presenter self-assessments where all attendees rate themselves on a scale of one to ten in twenty categories. Consistently the lowest rating occurs in the rehearsal category. Prior to the training session, less than 2 percent of the more than 5000 business professionals who have been through my course actually rehearse their presentation prior to performing it for an audience. Hopefully this percentage increases after the training! But this research helps explain why there are so few highly proficient speakers in business. "How do you get to Carnegie Hall?" asks the tourist. The cab driver replies, "Practice, practice, practice."

Speaking is like show business. Imagine buying a $200 orchestra-center seat to see *The Phantom of the Opera* on Broadway. At eight o'clock that evening the curtain rises as you eagerly await the first act. To your dismay the performers walk on stage, miss their cues, flub their lines, and the orchestra is out of tune. As an audience member, you would likely be shocked and disappointed, not to mention deserving a refund. A presentation is similar. Based upon average executive salaries, it costs the average company the same "ticket price" for one of their high-level leaders to spend an hour sitting in a presentation. As the speaker, if I'm not well-rehearsed and prepared, I not only disappoint my paying audience, but I miss a huge opportunity to influence key decision-makers, promote myself and my cause, and possibly win the corporate equivalent of a Tony award. One or two dress rehearsals can *significantly* improve the likelihood of success.

Regarding other common pitfalls, I went straight to the source. Over the years, I've polled hundreds of audience members and asked what they liked and didn't like about the presenter or speaker. At the top of the list is a monotone voice or monotonous delivery style. Audiences despise boredom. They really want to feel a connection with the presenter and experience his or her enthusiasm and passion. For this reason, please don't read from a script. There's no faster way to lose an audience's attention. Instead, look them in the eye and speak conversationally using a few bullet points on a card or slide.

Of course, not knowing your audience is the biggest mistake. Listeners will forgive a multitude of other errors if they believe you care about them and have taken the time to get to know them. And they'll love you if you help them be more successful. On the other hand, they can be unforgiving and downright angry if the presenter wastes their time, delivers irrelevant information, and fails to deliver value. So, my adage is, "Show 'em you know 'em!"

Many audience members used the phrase "winging it" as something they don't like. This is evidenced by lack of preparation, rambling, disorganization, apologies, no road map, and not knowing the audience. Several times I've advised unprepared clients to stay home if they haven't done their homework versus showing up at the customer site and "winging it." No impression is better than leaving a bad impression.

Another big complaint is the failure to speak on the audience's level of understanding. This may entail either speaking over their heads with specialized minutia and jargon unknown to the audience or speaking too broadly and not offering enough detail to add value.

Another pet peeve is failure to stay on topic and or belaboring the point. Sometimes these problems occur when an audience member asks a simple question and the presenter's answer becomes a fifteen-minute tangent, versus the recommended sixty-second response. Other times, the speaker simply dwells on a topic too long and fails to recognize his audience's signals to move on.

Poorly designed and overused slides are a common mishap. It's critical for every presenter to remember this truism: You are your most important visual aid. Slides support the speaker; they do not replace the speaker. Please avoid what I call PowerPoint on steroids—too much muscle for the message. Too many slides confuse the audience and usually rush the speaker. A good rule of thumb is to speak one and a half to two minutes on each slide. So, a twenty-minute presentation would typically have no more than ten to twelve content slides. Also, avoid the "eye-charts"—too much copy in a microscopic font. The guideline is 6x6—no more than six lines of copy at six words per line—phrases only, not full sentences.

According to my audience surveys, these represent the seven top pitfalls to avoid: lack of rehearsal and preparation, monotone voice, not knowing the audience, winging it, not speaking on their level, belaboring the point, and poorly designed slides. Oh, there are more for sure, but we'd all hear a big sigh of relief from audiences everywhere if we just brushed up on these seven.

Wright

In your interviews with audience members, what are the top traits they liked most in successful presenters and speakers?

Price

In most research, including my own, enthusiasm is most often the top-ranked quality. Whatever the setting—a motivational keynote, sales presentation, operational review, technical report, dinner meeting speech, sermon, or media interview—the listener is most impressed by the speaker's passion for the topic—a sparkle in the eye, variety in the voice, conviction for the content, and pep in the step, (i.e., enthusiasm). One of my favorite quotes is by John Wesley: "Catch on fire with enthusiasm and people will come for miles to watch you burn!" Enthusiasm is contagious, so when you have it your audience catches it.

Now why do you suppose *enthusiasm* is the most important? Because it prevents boredom? Helps entertain the audience? Engages them? Makes them feel good? Yes. But more importantly, enthusiasm conveys sincerity. And sincerity is an equally significant ingredient in successful speaking. Generally people do not muster up the energy to get excited about something unless they sincerely believe in it. And to be sure, the speaker must show he or she believes in the message before the audience will believe in it. By giving the speech with gusto, you actually prove your sincerity to the audience, which helps them believe in you and what you are saying.

The root meaning of the word "sincere" is worth noting and sheds light on why audience members value it so highly. In the ancient Roman marketplace where clay vases were made and sold, the storekeeper would often cleverly take his damaged or broken vases and patch the cracks with clear wax, then sell them to unsuspecting customers at full price. Of course, buyers did not want inferior goods, so the savvy customers always asked for a vase "without wax." The Latin word for "without" is "*sine*." The Latin word for "wax" is "*cere*;" they wanted a *sine-cere* vase—a genuine, real, whole product, without deceptive trickery. Nothing has changed. Today's audiences want the same thing—a *sincere* speaker who is honest, authentic, and true, without slick tactics. This is why my mantra to clients is: Be your natural wonderful self . . . at your very best.

Other qualities audience members rate highly include audience focus—as we've already discussed, they want above all to have their needs and issues specifically addressed. People want to know how much you care about *them*, before they care how much you know about the topic.

Approachability is high on the list. Listeners want to feel a connection with their speaker and this begins by being friendly and approachable. Consider arriving early to meet and chat with attendees ahead of time. Learn and use some of their names and use audience examples from the platform. It's also great to warmly welcome questions and comments, if appropriate. Interact with your listeners throughout the presentation and make yourself available afterward.

Good storytelling is a favorite! The ability to tell a good story makes a business presentation come to life. It's one of the best ways to make a connection with your listeners and the benefits abound. It captures the attention of your audience, makes you more "human," takes advantage of your own natural style and personality, makes abstract concepts clearer and more interesting, shares applicable lessons, prompts internal reflection, serves as a great medium for natural humor, and capitalizes on the way humans learn and remember information.

A great example of a dynamic storyteller is my client Pat. As the new president of a major corporation, she initially thought her primary role was to inform her audiences about the company's performance and industry standing. Pat prepared copious slides, triple-checked the numbers, and rehearsed the data. No one had better command of content than Pat. Her efforts were highly admirable, but the audience evaluations were consistently flat—something was missing. Pat soon discovered that her role as a leader was not only to inform but also to *inspire*.

During the dress rehearsal for a major presentation, I turned on my video camera and proceeded to have a friendly conversation. "Pat, someone told me you have three beautiful sons at home. Please tell me a little bit about each of them." All of a sudden, Pat's face lit up with a smile. Her eyes sparkled, her gestures became animated, her voice sounded more confident, and she moved and spoke fluidly with passion. When she saw herself on tape, that's all it took. She knew that was the inspiring delivery style an audience wanted and deserved. A few weeks later in a company-wide presentation, Pat told a heart-warming story about proudly watching her athletic teenage son round the bases with a confident stride. She then likened his confidence and success to her employees' momentum as she congratulated them for covering all the bases of the business. Her listeners loved it.

Over the course of two years, Pat has worked harder than anyone I know on presentation success. As a result, she is now a prominent and frequent speaker in her industry. Today, Pat's company is the number one solution provider in its business, she has received numerous prestigious awards, and her audience evaluations top the charts. And you can be sure that in every speech, Pat tells a story about her sons—to her listeners' delight.

Brevity is another quality valued especially by executive audiences. A whopping 98 percent of the senior executives I interviewed want the presenter to be concise and to the point. They typically loathe rambling, ambling, verbose presentation styles. Voltaire had it right: "The secret of being a bore is to tell everything." Ann unfortunately tried to tell everything and it was stunting her career. Her CEO said to her, "Ann, it takes you thirty minutes to say what ought to be said in three. Get to the point or get out of my office!" That's a pretty strong but clear message!

Ann and I went to work on what I've termed "Pyramid Speaking." You frame your thoughts in the shape of a pyramid with the headline at the very top (e.g., the big idea, key take-away, main point, thirty-second sound-bite). Then, you strategically outline the next most important points with key supporting details. Finally, you outline what you would like to say, if time permits. Ann was doing it backward—she began her presentations with everything she would like to say and eventually arrived to the main point.

Three weeks later, she presented to her CEO with a very different outcome. "Bob, in respect of your time I'll be brief. Sales in the East are down this quarter by 25 percent. Based on the three-part contingency plan I've put into place, our business unit will still make quota for the year. Our first step is—" Bob reported to me, "Wow! What a difference." Due in part to her new ability to clearly, concisely, and confidently communicate with her CEO and other key leaders, Ann was promoted to executive vice president within six months.

In addition, audiences love organization—it helps the brain categorize and store the information for optimum retention. For this reason, I advise speakers to stick with the "Tell 'Em" principle. "Tell them what you're going to tell them, tell them, then tell them what you told them." Of course there are exceptions to every rule, but in general, both the audience and speaker benefit mightily by having a clear opening including an intro, attention-getter, purpose statement, and roadmap that's telling them what you're going to tell them. Next, the main body that tells them has three to five key points with relevant supporting data and transition statements. Then, a solid close which tells them what you told them, including a clear summary and call to action.

Finally, audiences ultimately want knowledge. The president of a large consumer electronics company said me, "If someone's in my office presenting, they'd better tell me something I don't know. Otherwise, why am I paying them?" Francis Bacon believed, "Knowledge is power," and so do audiences. Give them relevant, substantive content and teach them something they don't know. Nothing builds credibility faster than knowing your stuff and using it to help your audience.

I suppose we could name this list of what audiences like the "Top Tips for Talented Talkers:" enthusiasm, sincerity, approachability, audience-focus, storytelling, brevity, organization, and knowledge. Similar to the previous list, there are more that could be mentioned, but if we strive to practice these eight tips each time we face our audiences, they'll be delighted and we'll experience a new level of speaking success.

Wright

In this hi-tech age, has technology and the Internet reduced our need to communicate face-to-face?

Price

On the contrary, technology has *increased* the need for face-to-face interaction. Ultimately, people do business with people, not electronics, technology, or products and certainly not with e-mail or voice mail. Long-term success is based on building relationships and you can't build meaningful relationships without meaningful face-to-face communication. Even the most successful and avid fans of hi-tech believe this. As Michael Dell, founder and chairman of Dell Computers says, "Our business is about technology, yes. But it's primarily about customer relationships."

Several years ago, the president of the world's largest employer said to me, "Darlene, no one's going to buy a ten million dollar product from someone they haven't met." He's right. Despite all of the new high-tech alternatives, an effective in-person sales presentation is still the single most powerful marketing tool in use today because people buy from people. And despite the use of impressive slides, multi-media, or efficient "webinars," your most effective selling tool is your face-to-face ability to persuasively communicate and build relationships.

There's no doubt that technology has given us powerful tools to stay in touch and improve productivity, but not without consequences. Researchers at Stanford report a definite link between increased Internet usage and increased social isolation—at home and on the job. It's ironic that the world is more connected than ever before but people spend less time in person with those they care about. Unfortunately, quantity of communication seems to have replaced quality.

The bright side of this negative trend is that the personal touch is now a key differentiator—the hand-written note, the personal visit, the phone call versus e-mail. You can capitalize on this fact to boost your career and differentiate yourself. We laugh when we hear Woody Allen say that 80 percent of success is showing up. But when showing up helps you stand head and shoulders above the competition, he's right!

Two years ago, a client of mine won a multi-million-dollar deal because she and her team showed up in person at the prospect's office. Since the request for proposal allowed electronic submissions, the other vendors conveniently e-mailed their presentation. Sue, on the other hand, telephoned the Chief Information Officer and requested the privilege of meeting him face-to-face. The next day, the team flew across the country, persuasively presented their proposal in person, dined with the decision makers, and walked away with a verbal agreement—before the competitors' electronic proposals had even been read!

I believe that as long as human beings are involved, the need for high-touch far outweighs the convenience of high-tech. Perhaps John Naisbitt, author of the best-selling books *Megatrends* and *Re-*

inventing the Corporation, says it best, "The most exciting breakthroughs of the twenty-first century will not occur because of technology, but because of an expanding concept of what it means to be human."

Wright

We've discussed the presentation and public speaking aspect of this skill set. What about interpersonal communications? What does it take to be successful dealing with colleagues and customers one-on-one day after day?

Price

So often, people with the highest IQs or most impressive resumes don't land the top jobs. The answer almost always lies in interpersonal skills. A more encompassing term for this crucial area is called emotional intelligence, or EI. In his best-selling books, *Emotional Intelligence* and *Working with Emotional Intelligence*, Dr. Daniel Goleman's research reveals that the single most important factor in success is not IQ, advanced degrees, specialized knowledge, or technical expertise, but the quality called "Emotional Intelligence," which means you can accurately read and effectively manage the emotions, motivations, and behaviors of yourself and others during social interactions.

This, of course, is challenging for most of us. I'm reminded of a *Peanuts* cartoon where Linus Van Pelt says, "I love humanity; its people I can't stand." The competencies involved in Emotional Intelligence give us the "security blanket" to not only love humanity but also get along with the 6.6 billion people who comprise it. When learned and applied, this interpersonal suite of skills gives us the ability to initiate and sustain a meaningful, healthy, productive relationship—with ourselves and others. It shows you how to handle yourself and others in ways that build trust, manage conflict, negotiate win-win outcomes, create harmony, and foster teamwork.

Many great leaders of the past may not have called it emotional intelligence, but they sure learned how to practice it and understood its importance. For example, Ronald Regan, who earned the title The Great Communicator, once said, "Be more concerned about making others feel good about themselves than you are making them feel good about you." Theodore Roosevelt, who was awarded the Nobel Peace Prize and Medal of Honor wrote, "The most important ingredient in the formula of success is knowing how to get along with people." And Indira Gandhi, Prime Minister of India for two terms, believed, "You cannot shake hands with a clenched fist." I believe this new measurement of success—the Emotional Quotient or EQ—comprises the key competencies we need to be successful at work, at home, and in the world.

Wright

How exactly is *emotional* intelligence linked to success in the workplace?

Price

The word "emotion" in a business context tends to be misleading, doesn't it? A corporation prides itself in being rational, logical, and judicious.

However, if you think about it, emotions always exist—we always feel something. I think one of the most important lessons I've learned from the talented leaders and mentors in my life is that when dealing with people you must remember that you're not dealing with creatures of logic, but creatures of emotion. This doesn't mean that reason and logic are not present and crucial—they are, of course. But emotions are the gatekeeper. Research has shown that typically people make decisions based on emotions first, then look for the logic, rationale, and data to support those decisions. Emotions are what move us to action, and if we want to move others and ourselves to action, we must first and foremost consider what fuels that action—the emotions. And the basic four that fill our offices, homes, and world are: mad, sad, glad, and scared.

We must first manage and respond appropriately to the emotions—ours and others'—in order to optimize our ability to relate interpersonally. If you think about it, emotions are often the root cause within and among people that will make or break deals, adopt or reject change, increase or decrease employee turnover, inspire or impair teamwork, win or lose the big promotion, like or dislike a co-worker.

For example, one of my new clients, Dan, is an executive vice president in a Fortune 100 company. He has an IQ of 132 and is considered intellectually gifted. There is no doubt he commands an impressive mental capacity to reason, plan, solve problems, think abstractly, give and execute commands, comprehend ideas, and learn. However, at his last performance review he was dismayed to read the results of his 360-degree feedback assessment, a tool that gathers information about a person from his or her circle of colleagues—boss, employees, teams, peers, and customers. Across the board, he received unfavorable ratings in the area of interpersonal communication and relationships, with descriptors such as non-collaborative, defensive, a poor listener, blaming, and insensitive. No wonder his department had the highest turnover and his teams the lowest productivity rating in the company. As a result, the president did not promote Dan to the higher-paying general manager position, even though he was the obvious next-in-line candidate for the job. Despite his intelligence and credentials, the lack of people skills was limiting his success.

But there's hope. As Dan and his circle of colleagues are discovering, the Emotional Quotient or EQ, is teachable and learnable. He telephoned me recently to exclaim, "Someone actually called me a likeable guy today!" And fortunately, unlike IQ, which on average tops out as a teenager and is stable over a person's lifetime, EQ can continue to develop and improve. Though Dan still prides himself in being rational, logical, and judicious, he's adding another type of intelligence to his repertoire—one that makes him people-smart. It is sure to land him the advancement and recognition he deserves, not to mention happier healthier relationships.

Wright

Earlier, you mentioned the key competencies of emotional intelligence. What are they and how do they apply to success in business?

Price

In a nutshell, there are two main areas of emotional intelligence. First, *Personal Competence* determines how we manage ourselves. This includes three self-checks: self-awareness, which accurately assesses one's own strengths and weaknesses; self-regulation, which keeps disruptive emotions and impulses in check; and self-motivation, which cultivates the drive, commitment, initiative, and optimism necessary for overcoming obstacles and reaching goals.

The second area is *Social Competence*, better known as relationship skills. It determines how we manage others and handle interpersonal relationships. Social competencies include, for example, empathy—an awareness of others' feelings, needs, and concerns. Empathy enables a person to sense others' moods and perspectives, and take an active interest in their concerns. Social skills are also crucial, which involve listening actively and sending persuasive messages, getting along well with others, working with and leading others toward shared goals, negotiating and resolving disagreements, and initiating or managing change.

Now, how do we develop and apply these personal and social competencies to improve relationships and advance our career? Consider my client Rick. One of his company's largest customers became dissatisfied and disgruntled, evidenced by the 2.5 customer satisfaction rating (ten is the highest). The products didn't work properly, shipments were delayed, they were losing customers, service and support were insufficient, and they hadn't seen their sales rep in months. Of the four basic emotions, this customer was feeling mad, sad, and scared with little or no glad. Needless to say, they were ready to jump ship, cut their losses, and cancel their contract. That's when Rick took over. His boss gave him the opportunity to solve the problem, so Rick and I went to work on a plan to win back the customer.

We first had to consider the fact that a human being's most basic and important emotional need is to feel heard and understood. At the time, Rick couldn't do anything about the product problems—that was engineering's job. He couldn't do anything about service and support—that was a staffing issue. However, Rick could listen. He could make sure his customer felt heard and understood. For six months, Rick met with his customer weekly face-to-face. He asked questions, listened to complaints, wrote copious notes, toured the facility, took responsibility for the mishaps, kept his cool, and resolved disagreements. Rick was relentless in winning back the customer. After more than twenty visits, nothing significant had changed about the product and support problems, yet the new customer satisfaction rating was 7.5! The score tripled because the customer felt heard and understood. That was goal number one.

The second goal was to fix the product and support problems. Rick tactfully persisted until he met face-to-face with the people within his company who could solve his customer's problems. He presented a persuasive case and got the issues resolved ahead of schedule. One year later, the customer satisfaction rating now stands at 9.8. Armed with a high EQ and a caring attitude, Rick not only made his company millions of dollars by salvaging the account, he exceeded his own quota by selling them numerous additional solutions.

Rick is a good example of how emotional intelligence is good for business. When we apply both the personal and social competencies to help ourselves and others succeed, everyone wins. I've seen the interpersonal power of emotional intelligence not only boost careers and customer satisfaction ratings; I've seen it prevent corporate law suits, reduce turnover, improve operational efficiency, win sales, and create harmonious productive teams.

Wright

What are a top ten best practices that improve one's emotional intelligence and produce more interpersonal success?

Price

Here are my top ten best practices:

1. *Be positive.* First of all, smile at people and be pleasant. A client who is the general manager of a major hotel chain displays this Chinese proverb on his desk: "A man without a smiling face should not open a shop." Try this: For just one day, wear a cheerful countenance and give every living creature you meet a smile. Talk health, happiness, and prosperity to others and notice the difference in your own outlook and those around you. You'll quickly discover that attitude determines altitude! The positive energy you radiate will draw opportunities and others to you like metal to a magnet.
2. *Show appreciation to others.* Many of us don't realize the power we have to make someone's day. The willingness to put appreciation into words is all it takes. Find the good in the people around you and then tell them about it. Be generous with sincere praise and kind words of encouragement. If you say "thank you" often, encourage others, and help them reach their goals, they will love you for it and give you their best. Those who bring sunshine into the lives of others cannot keep it from themselves.
3. *Show interest in others.* Try the 80/20 rule and watch your relational skills skyrocket. Ask thoughtful questions and actively listen 80 percent of the time; talk the other 20 percent. Dale Carnegie once sat beside a New York gossip columnist at a dinner event. To stay out of trouble, he decided he would do nothing the entire evening but ask her questions and listen. The next morning she wrote, ". . . and Mr. Dale Carnegie is by far the best conversationalist I have ever met!" You can be, too.

Observe what's going on in the lives of your co-workers, customers, friends, and loved ones. Celebrate their accomplishments and acknowledge special occasions. Likewise, express concern during difficult times and extend your sympathy over an illness or death.

4. *Practice empathy.* Empathy takes "interest in others" to a higher level of emotional intelligence. Carolyn, a client in the banking industry, actually hung a pair of leather moccasins in her office to remind her of the ancient proverb, "Walk a mile in their moccasins." The symbol was a public commitment to step inside the shoes of others and see issues from their side. Carolyn learned to study their facial expressions and body language, listen to their tone of voice, rate of speech, and choice of words. She acquired the ability to get an immediate sense of how they felt on the inside and respond appropriately. As a result, her performance reviews carried the top ratings in the company on listening skills and interpersonal effectiveness.
5. *Listen actively.* When interacting with others, don't multi-task. Stop what you're doing, face them fully using good eye contact, and give them your undivided attention. Perhaps the first duty of leadership is to listen. A general during the Civil War said of Abe Lincoln, "He listens so hard it exhausts me." Concentrate on the person, listen for meaning, and check with the speaker to verify and clarify what you heard. Maintain eye contact and open body language. By listening actively to those around you, you not only learn, you increase mutual understanding, build trust, resolve conflict, and set the tone for openness and honesty. Plus, as we learned from Rick, you fulfill the most basic human need—the need to feel heard and understood.
6. *Communicate clearly.* In the interpersonal arena, we only have two ways to communicate: verbal and non-verbal. Now here's a question: which one would you guess carries the most message impact? I ask my workshop attendees this question and many of them answer correctly: nonverbal. Then I ask, "By what percentage?" In all my years of training, no one guesses high enough the first time around. Studies actually show nonverbal can carry as much as 93 percent of your message impact, with words

alone carrying only 7 percent. Wow! The key take-away there is to realize *how* you say something is much more memorable and persuasive than *what* you say. For this reason, pay close attention to your body language and voice tone (the how), and spend less energy on scrutinizing and word-smithing (the what). Quality content is definitely important but it'll fall on deaf ears if the delivery doesn't carry it. For presentations, meetings, and important phone calls, make notes ahead of time and practice aloud what you'll say. Also, avoid blurting out whatever comes to mind or making impulsive comments to people. Bite your tongue and think first. Ask yourself, "Is this comment helpful? Will it serve a higher good? Does it get me closer to my desired outcome?" Considered, clear, and confident communication conveys leadership, intelligence, and confidence. It also fosters better relationships and an executive presence.

7. *Project a professional image.* I never thought of William Shakespeare as an image consultant but let's take his advice anyway: "The apparel oft proclaims the man." Studies show that people perceive your work clothes as a symbol of your competence. Advertise your capabilities, credibility, and quality by looking professional and capable. A good rule of thumb is to dress for the job you want, not the job you have. And always appear well groomed. Know that people will look at your face and neck first. Look neat from head to toe with a neat current haircut and style, high-quality but simple jewelry, smooth hands, manicured nails and polished shoes. And be sure your handshake consists of a full, firm handclasp, web-to-web. (Please, none of those weak, limp, or dead fish handshakes!) Pump up and down firmly two or three times. Smile, maintain eye contact, and learn the person's name.
8. *Foster teamwork and value diversity.* Find ways to bring people together and cultivate opportunities through different kinds of people. I remember my grandmother always telling me that what makes a beautiful flower garden is variety. Create an environment that honors differences, encourages collaboration, and awards teamwork. Treat everyone equally and don't play favorites.

Avoid talking about others behind their backs. If people see you as someone with integrity, fairness, and who has respect for others, they will trust you. Also, solicit feedback and follow up on other people's input. And remember to praise your teammates—a pat on the back is only a few inches up from a kick in the pants, but it's miles ahead in results!

9. *Facilitate conflict resolution.* Blessed are the peacemakers, as the verse goes. As a leader, go beyond bringing people together. Strive to resolve damaging disagreements and gain a win/win outcome. I love Mark Twain's observation that if two people agree on everything, one of them is unnecessary! Indeed, disagreements are often needed for healthy balance and perspective. But when conflict risks jeopardizing a relationship, step in if appropriate and play the neutral role of facilitator and mediator. By taking on such a leadership role, you will garner respect and admiration from colleagues and preserve precious resources—known as relationships.
10. *Use humor.* It's been said that laughter is, after speech, the chief thing that holds society together. One of my clients sure believes it holds her company together. She created a volunteer position that anyone in the firm can fill called the "Director of Fun and Laughs." Employees have enjoyed it so much that there's a two-year waiting list for the role. Not only are Dianne's stories both heartwarming and hilarious, she has measurable results of improved employee morale, gained higher productivity, and harmonious teamwork. People love to laugh—don't be afraid to show your sense of humor and let your wit shine. It lowers communication barriers, creates a relaxed open atmosphere, plus you have more fun!

And there's my top ten list of "Interpersonal Best Practices." The quality of our lives is measured in large part by the quality of our relationships. The same can be said for the quality of our companies. The concept of product quality is central to successful businesses—everyday improvements are made via design, manufacturing, layout, processes, and procedures. My hope and best counsel is that we apply the same level of energy and focus to improving the day-to-day interactions with the people around us.

Wright

What message would you like to leave us with?

Price

You can probably tell from our conversation that I like quotes! So allow me to close with one. "When your message benefits others, you not only have a right to speak, you have an obligation to do so." I thank Eleanor Roosevelt for that advice because when I read it over two decades ago, my *desire* to speak, train, and coach was ignited with *duty*. Desire brings delight and satisfaction when delivering a message, but duty gives it purpose, passion and power. And my message is this: there is only one of you in the world—just one—and if the people around you do not hear what you have to say in the unique way in which you say it, then something has been lost. Don't die with the music or the message in you. At work, at home, in the community and the world, please speak up and speak out. Claim your power and present yourself. Present your message, services, products, company and convictions to the world around you. If you don't know how, I promise you can learn. If you do know how, please serve as a role model for others. And make relationships a priority.

Effective face-to-face speaking and interpersonal relationship skills will not only get you noticed, remembered, and promoted more often and more quickly than any other skill set, it helps ensure you get more of what you want and deserve in life. By acquiring these abilities, you can rest assured that you possess the number one skill in business today and begin enjoying a whole new level of success, personally and professionally.

About the Author

DARLENE PRICE, internationally acclaimed executive speech coach, is the president of Well Said! Inc., an organization dedicated to helping others speak and communicate more effectively. Chief officers and senior executives in the Fortune 100 and Global 2000 rely on Darlene for their speaking success, and she has trained over 5000 business professionals around the world. As the recipient of nine Telly Awards and one Emmy for outstanding corporate presentations, Darlene is a frequent expert source for the media, and conducts group workshops, private coaching, and keynote addresses.

Darlene Price
President
Well Said! Inc.
P.O. Box 888346
Atlanta, GA 30356
Phone: 678.361.7004
E-mail: darleneprice@wellsaid.com
www.wellsaid.com

Chapter 7

Bud Bilanich

THE INTERVIEW

David Wright (Wright)

Today we're talking with Dr. Bud Bilanich. His pragmatic approach to business, life and the business of life has earned him the title of "The Common Sense Guy" and has made him one of the most sought after speakers, consultants, and executive coaches in the United States. Dr. Bilanich's work focuses on improving the performance of individuals, teams, and entire organizations. Bud is Harvard educated but he has a commonsense, no-nonsense approach to his work that stretches back to his roots in the steel country of Western Pennsylvania.

Bud, welcome to *Speaking of Success*.

Dr. Bud Bilanich (Bilanich)

Thank you so much for inviting me, David. It's great to chat with you.

Wright

So they call you the "Common Sense Guy." Why is that?

Bilanich

I've been doing this kind of work—organization effectiveness and executive coaching—for close to thirty years now. Over that time I've developed a great appreciation for the power of common sense. Sad to say, very often people don't use common sense in their day-to-day work and in their businesses.

A few years ago I decided that common sense was something that was missing in business in America. I also decided I would begin focusing my practice on helping people apply their common sense to solve a lot of complex problems they face.

Wright

What are some of the biggest mistakes businesspeople make when it comes to common sense?

Bilanich

I think there are two of them. The first one is falling for fads. If you look just at the management literature and the hundreds of direct mail ads that come across your desk and your e-mail in-box these days, you find all kinds of offers and solicitations. They all say essentially the same thing: "try this program, it'll solve all your problems," or "here is the answer to all of your difficult questions," or "if you only do what I suggest, and follow my particular program exactly as I've laid it out, all of your troubles will go away."

I think that most of our knowledge concerning business and life success is built on some basic, commonsense principles. Most new programs and most fads are just these commonsense principles dressed up in some new clothes and new language.

One of the things that I try to do is help people cut through all of the "noise," get down to the basic ideas behind these programs, and help them apply logical, commonsense solutions to the issues they face.

The second problem is one of application. Common sense is called common sense because it is most often common knowledge—most people know the right thing to do in most situations. Often, though, the commonsense thing to do takes a lot of work. I believe it was Thomas Edison who said, "Opportunity is missed by most people because it is dressed in overalls and looks like work."

The same thing is true with common sense. It too, usually comes dressed in overalls and looks like hard work. Many people know exactly what they should do but they don't do it because it's difficult or time consuming or they have to make a commitment or it takes a lot of effort and energy. So instead, they look for something that is easy and quick on the surface. They usually end up creating more problems for themselves than if they'd just bitten the bullet and done what they knew was the correct thing to do in the first place.

Wright

You write a blog called "Common Sense Guy." What made you decide to write it and how did you get started?

Bilanich

First of all I am very fascinated by technology and how—to borrow a phrase from Thomas Friedman—it is flattening the world. I like the notion of blogs that allow people to communicate directly with others via the World Wide Web. It's fascinating to me that I have so many readers outside of the U.S. in places like India, Australia, Japan, and Europe.

There's a real opportunity with a blog to be able to communicate ideas about common sense. On my blog, www.commonsenseguy.com, I take issues that I find by reading *USA Today, The Wall Street Journal, The New York Times,* or the local paper in the town where I have some business, and point out common sense in action. More often though, I find myself describing where people have not used their common sense and it has resulted in some problems. For example, did Jeff Skilling and Ken Lay really think they could get away with it? On my blog, I take real world situations and then show how people could have used their common sense to do a better in handling them.

Wright

You've worked with some pretty big companies—GM, Glaxo SmithKline, Citicorp, Aetna, and Philadelphia Electric, as well as some small companies. Where do you find more applied common sense?

Bilanich

In general I find it in the smaller companies. That's not to say that the big companies don't have people who use common sense. But in many large companies, I often find that the culture sometimes mitigates against applied common sense. Earlier I mentioned that people will jump on the latest fad bandwagon. All too often in large companies I find this type of scenario: Someone in a senior leadership position hears that Jack Welch really thinks that Six Sigma is the latest and greatest thing and that it really worked well for GE. This leader says to himself or herself, "If it worked there, it should work here." All of a sudden, people are into doing Six Sigma projects. If the executive had dug a little deeper into the organization, he or she might have found out that there were a lot of people who were doing a lot of continuous improvement work similar to Six Sigma already. Mandating the use of a specific program like Six Sigma or worse yet, a specific vendor caused a lot of upset and problems and undid a lot of good work that had been going on.

Also, I find that because there are more layers in big companies, there are more opportunities for messages to get confused as they move through the organization. The intent of senior executives often gets caught in what I call "the middle management black hole."

Smaller companies—more entrepreneurial companies—usually have fewer layers. And the people paying the bills are also the ones making the decisions. That's one of the main reasons I think you see more applied common sense in smaller companies.

Wright

You say that your job description is to enhance the performance of individuals, teams, and organizations. So how do you do it?

Bilanich

I basically do three things: I'm an executive coach and work a lot with individuals, coaching them on enhancing their personal and leadership effectiveness; I consult with a lot of teams, helping improve their effectiveness, teamwork, and performance. I also work with companies undergoing major change. Lately, I have spent a lot of time doing merger and acquisition integration work.

I have identified and created models such as: what it takes to have a successful career, what it takes to be a successful leader, what it takes to run a successful team, and what it takes to run a successful organization. These are all based on commonsense principles.

I begin work with all of my clients by finding out exactly where they are in relation to, and how well they're performing when viewed from, the perspective of these commonsense models. Then I help them find ways to build on where they're performing well and ways to overcome some of the problems they have where they're not performing as well as they could be.

Wright

Let's talk about individuals. How do you help them in their careers?

Bilanich

I've developed a model I call "Career Star Power." Like most stars, it has five points: self-confidence, personal impact, performance, communication skills, and interpersonal confidence.

I help each individual with whom I work identify how well he or she is doing relative to each points of the star. I find that some people do very well in three or four of them and might be lacking in one or two. Others may be extremely good at one and could use some help on the other four. My idea is to break things into some bite-sized commonsense chunks, take things one at a time, and help people improve until they become the stars they are destined to be.

Wright

Tell me more about these points. Let's start with self-confidence.

Bilanich

Self-confidence is the foundation of every successful career. If you don't believe in yourself—if you don't have a strong belief that you can succeed and will succeed, you're not going to succeed. One of the biggest blocks to self-confidence is fear. People are afraid to fail so they don't want to try. Some people would rather be in a situation where they don't do something and therefore they can say they didn't fail. Successful people actually do something. Sometimes they take their lumps. But, sometimes they succeed. Mike Ditka sums it up pretty well—"Success isn't permanent and failure isn't fatal.

I'm a big fan of the Teddy Roosevelt arena quote where he talks about how he admires the person inside the arena—the one whose face is marred with dust and sweat and gets up time after time and keeps trying. That's one of the things I work with my clients on. I help them identify their fears, what's holding them back from moving forward in their careers, and then I help them use this knowledge as a springboard to develop their self-confidence.

Wright

What do you mean by the term "personal impact"?

Bilanich

Personal impact is how people think of you. Do they think of you as a person who is dynamic, in charge, self-confident, and one who knows what he or she is doing? Do they think of you as bumbling, confused, and fearful? Or, worse yet, do they not think of you at all?

People with personal impact are those who look people in the eye, smile, and shake hands. They know how to dress appropriately for the work situation. They have good manners. They can engage people they don't know very well in interesting and meaningful conversations.

It's very interesting, I've been finding that over the past few years, as we've become more casual in business, more and more clients are coming to me and asking if I can help their young people understand a little bit more about professionalism and dress. One of the commonsense points I always make with these young people is simple: "Your organization may have a business casual policy, but remember that 'business' is the first word in 'business casual.'" That means some commonsense things like sneakers and flip-flops are not appropriate office wear—unless you're working at Google. I've found that most people, not just young people, can enhance their personal impact by spending a little more time on their personal appearance.

Explaining simple table manners is another way that I help people enhance their personal impact. As families are more fragmented—both parents working, kids at lots of after-school activities—family dinnertime isn't what it once was. Many people don't learn basic table manners at home at the family dinner table as they once did. Simple things like knowing that the water glass is on the right and the bread plate is on the left can save you from embarrassment when you sit down to a business meal.

All of these things roll into what I refer to as creating a positive personal impact. A positive personal impact results in people both remembering you and remembering you in a positive way.

Wright

Another point on the star is performance. How does that work in your Career Star Power model?

Bilanich

It comes down again to common sense. No matter how confident you are, and how well you present yourself, you still have to deliver the goods. If you don't do your job well, people will come to see you as an "empty suit."

Performance is about setting goals and achieving them; doing it today, tomorrow, the next day, this year, next year, and the year after. What it really comes down to is that performance is being able to set goals and meet them, exceed them, and then set higher goals and meet and exceed those.

Wright

So what are the factors that make up good communication skills?

Bilanich

Communication is about how you deal with the rest of the world. You need to know how to write well and that's not just for reports, it's for things like e-mails too. I think people often forget that e-mails are business correspondence. They don't spend enough time doing some of the small things like running it through spell-check or re-reading it to make sure it reads well and that they have all of their ducks in a row—the tenses are all the same, they're not confusing first person with third person, and that they're using active voice. I help a lot of people learn how to write better.

Effective communicators know how to manage conversations and make presentations. Standing in front of a group of people and getting your point across in a persuasive manner is an important career enhancing ability. It's one of the easiest ways to get noticed and recognized as a player by important people in organizations.

When people think about presentations, particularly those who have a little stage fright, they're overwhelmed. I break down making, developing, and delivering a powerful presentation into a few commonsense steps. Most people tell me that once they see the commonsense steps in the presentation process, they can master them—one small chunk at a time. The next thing they know, they're not only good presenters they're confident presenters.

Wright

It's interesting to note that you indicated "interpersonal competence" rather than skills on the fifth point of the star. What is the reason for using interpersonal competence instead of skills?

Bilanich

I think that one can have skills but not use them, so I think there is a difference between being interpersonally competent and interpersonally skilled. It's more than just a semantic difference. I really do believe that one has to be interpersonally competent. Competence is applied knowledge.

Interpersonally competent people build strong, lasting, trusting, mutually beneficial relationships with all the people in their life—their boss, coworkers, customers, or suppliers. I think you need to be able to build relationships that help people feel good about you. For example, if they know they're going to have to make a phone call and speak with you, you want them to look forward to it, not dread it.

In the end, yes you have to be self-confident, yes you have to know how to make a positive impact, yes you have to perform and have the skills necessary to write, engage in conversation, and make presentations, but more importantly, you have to be interpersonally competent. You have to have and use the ability to build positive relationships with the people around you. That's what makes for real career success.

Wright

You also work with teams. I've been booking speakers for sixteen years and I'd like to say that teams have gotten better since I've been doing that because there are more seminars, books, and CDs on teamwork; but it's very difficult. What makes for a high performing team?

Bilanich

In my opinion, there are three things you have to be concerned about if you're trying to develop a high performing team.

The first one is what I refer to as a purpose or charter. You have to clearly define what you're all about—why does the team exist? If you look at teams in a business environment, you'll find a variety of different kinds of teams. You have teams that work together all the time like a senior leadership team—the leadership team of a company or of a division of a company or the sales leadership team, or the leadership team of a manufacturing or logistics operation. That's one kind of a team.

Then there are project teams. These teams are pulled together for a short term to accomplish a project and then they disband. There are also cross function teams. In a lot of companies you'll find teams composed of research and development, manufacturing, and sales and marketing people. These folks often are at each other's throats so teams are formed with representatives from each of these different functions or departments to help them all work better together.

Lately, virtual teams have become a big thing. Technology has made it possible for people who aren't located in the same place to be able to work together as a team pretty effectively even though they don't see each other on a day-to-day basis.

Each of the types of teams I've mentioned needs a purpose or charter, and each of these statements will be quite different from one another. It all starts with the answer to two questions: "Why do we exist as a team? What are the outcomes we're hoping to accomplish?"

Wright

I've never heard the words "charter" and "purpose" used together before.

Bilanich

Really? I use them interchangeably when it comes to teamwork. The difference is that usually a team is in charge of its own destiny, a leadership team for example, defines its own purpose (and again, we're getting into semantics here). A team that has been convened or appointed by someone else, a cross function or project team for example, generally has a charter that has been given to them by the group or individual who convenes them.

I was recently working with a leadership team of a manufacturing organization. This included all of the plant managers in the U.S. for this company—there were about ten or twelve people who meet regularly. They decided that they wanted to focus on enhancing employee engagement. One of the things they wanted to do was put together a small survey to measure the engagement level of the people who worked in their organization. They created a small team whose charter was to develop this survey.

That's how I think of the difference between purpose and charter. Teams that control their own destiny choose their purpose. Teams that are designated by senior leaders are usually provided with a charter.

The net/net of all this is that whether you call it a purpose or charter, it's a statement that clearly defines the team's reason for existence. It provides members of the team an opportunity to occasionally say, "Wait a minute, is this what we should be doing? Is this in scope or out of scope for us as a team? Should we be focusing on this as a team?" That's the main value of a purpose or a charter—it sets the boundaries for what the team should or should not be working on.

Wright

Would you share with our readers what some of the internal factors are that lead to team success?

Bilanich

I think there are four:

The first is what I refer to as infrastructure—who's on the team. In some cases it's clearly defined because it consists of the leadership group of the departments in a company or in a unit of a company. In other cases it's not as clearly defined. You have to think about whom you really want to invite to make sure you have the proper representation to be able to get your work done.

Second, all effective teams have a set of ground rules by which they operate. I believe these should be explicit, not implicit. When I work with teams, one of the things I help them do first is get a clear picture of how they're going to work together and what the ground rules are. For example, there needs to be a negotiation of leadership—what the team expects of the leader, what the leader expects of the team—so that it's very clear in terms of how they're going to work together. In some cases there's a designated leader, in some cases leadership rotates among the members of the team. There are other issues such as how the meetings will be structured, how often the team will meet and so on. These are the nitty-gritty things you have to pay attention to if you're going to be able work well together as a team.

Third, there's trust—you have to have an open, honest, sharing climate that encourages participation. People need to feel free to speak their minds. Trust is a very, very important. It might be the most important internal factor when it comes to teamwork. Effective teams work at building trust.

Fourth, there's what I call spirit. The team has to believe in itself. Team members need to feel that they are going to be successful. It's the teamwork version of individual self-confidence. Effective teams really believe they're going to be successful, get the job done, and move forward.

Wright

Why are external relationships so important?

Bilanich

This is one of the places where I think my focus on teamwork is a little different from many other people who consult with teams. No team exists in a vacuum; it exists within an organizational structure or has been chartered for a specific purpose. All successful teams manage relationships with important constituencies outside the team.

It's important to identify these critical people and then to say, "What are they expecting of us? What are the success metrics that the person who chartered this team has in mind for this team? Let's make sure we align with our constituencies' success metrics."

I've seen a lot of teams get chartered to do a specific task and for some reason get sidetracked. The team members feel good about themselves because of what they've accomplished, but the people who were expecting a certain output from the team don't get that output. All of a sudden there is a conflict. The team members feel they have worked hard and accomplished a lot but they're not being recognized for their contribution when, in fact, their contribution wasn't what was expected of them from the people who put them together as a team in the first place. Over the years I've found that it's really important for teams to do an excellent job of meeting the expectations of key constituencies—especially the group or individual who chartered them.

Wright

So what do you think is the most critical thing to remember about an effective team?

Bilanich

Ultimately, it comes down to a clearly stated purpose or charter. Once that purpose is clearly stated and every member of the team gets on board and is willing to do what it takes to make the team successful, most other things will fall into place. A good purpose or charter statement provides an overarching reason for the team's existence, which in turn drives the commitment of everyone on the team and helps identify constituency expectations.

Wright

Let's move on to organizations. I know you've written a book titled *4 Secrets of High Performing Organizations.* What points do you make in your book?

Bilanich

First of all, the book came from my consulting work. I needed to develop a model so that I could understand what was happening in my clients' organizations—to be able to help them pinpoint problems and opportunities and then address them.

As I started working, it became clear to me that most successful organizations are pretty good at four things:

1. Clarity—They all have *clarity* of purpose and direction.
2. Commitment—They enlist the sincere *commitment* of everyone in the organization.
3. Execution—They skillfully *execute* the things that matter.
4. Relationships—They build mutually beneficial *relationships* with important outside constituencies.

Wright

Let's talk about clarity. What do you mean?

Bilanich

Just like a team, an organization needs to know where it's going. To me, this involves several major points. First there's mission. Successful organizations have a clear sense of what their mission is. I define mission as an organization's purpose and reason for existence. For example, your company is in the business of doing two things: booking speakers and helping speakers advance their message to the world. That's your clarity of purpose.

Then the clarity of purpose—this mission—needs to be translated into some strategy. How are we going to get there? What are we going to do? Where do we want to be in three to five years? You need to develop a strategic plan.

The strategic plan and the activities that are in that plan should filter all the way down to the individual performance objectives of people in even the lowest parts of the organization. I believe that it's important for companies, whether they be a two-person consulting company or a large Fortune 50 corporation, to be able to clearly say "this is why we're in business, this is where we're going, and this is what you (a division, department, an individual) need to do to help us get there."

It all starts with clarity of purpose. Clarity of purpose helps people understand what the big picture is and how they fit into that big picture.

Wright

When I think about clarity and purpose I think almost immediately of some of your writings about vision and values. It seems they go hand-in-hand. In my opinion you couldn't have one without the other.

Bilanich

Yes, I've written a book called *Using Values to Turn Vision into Reality.* Values are concepts and commitments that ground an organization. They help people understand how their organization does business. Values help people make decisions in ambiguous situations.

If we say, for example, that we value teamwork, one of the things that people should do is constantly ask themselves questions like, "Who needs to know what I'm doing? Who is going to be affected by this? Who are the people I need to be able to communicate with to let them know I've made this is decision?"

So, in organizations that truly value teamwork, people think from a teamwork perspective and ask those questions. In organizations that do not hold teamwork as a value, people don't naturally ask these questions.

Wright

What about commitment?

Bilanich

To me, commitment is all about getting people engaged with what you're doing as an organization. It starts even before you hire people. It starts with your selection process. Successful organizations make it hard to join them. When people do get invited to join, they feel good about themselves. Successful organizations do a good job with things like orientation and training. Their reward systems are set up to encourage performance and adherence to organizational values. By the way, I'm sure you know that there are both monetary and non-monetary rewards. You need to pay people a fair salary, but more importantly, people like to be rewarded for the contributions they make.

Leadership plays a big part of building commitment. One of the things I always say is that people don't leave companies—they leave bosses. You may have a great company but if you have a few bad leaders you will not gain the full commitment of your people, or worse yet, start to lose a lot of key people.

Commitment is doing whatever you can to ensure you have a group of engaged people who are excited about being in your company, who want to help the company go forward, and are committed to its goals and objectives.

Wright

Another one of your books is titled *Fixing Performance Problems.* Is this part of execution?

Bilanich

It is. I always say you have to skillfully execute the *things that matter*. You find the things that matter by going back to your clarity of purpose. One of the things you have to do when it comes to execution is take those plans, goals, and objectives and make sure you meet them or exceed them.

You also need to put into play some basic planning and control systems so that you're clear on what you are trying to accomplish and you have some way of measuring how well you're doing.

To me, execution comes down to the notion of operational excellence. To get to your question, if there are performance problems, leaders need to be able to find what those performance problems are and do the best they possibly can to fix them. Performance problems bog down the organization.

There also needs to be continuous improvement—taking a look at your business processes and saying, "How can we do this better, faster, cheaper? How can we be more productive in terms of what we're doing so that we can be successful here?"

Fixing problems is an important part of execution but I also believe that if you have effective planning and control systems and you build a culture of operational excellence, problems are more the exception rather than the norm.

Wright

You seem to be big on managing constituent relationships. Why do you focus so heavily on people outside of a team or organization?

Bilanich

I think that a lot of writers and people who do the kind of work I do somehow forget that any organization or any team exists in this larger social milieu and you need to pay attention to that. If you don't, you're going to run into problems.

Walmart provides an excellent example here. If you think about the clarity, commitment, execution, and relationships model, you'll see that Walmart is great on clarity and execution and terrible on commitment and relationships.

Walmart is incredibly clear on what they're all about—providing goods to customers at the lowest possible price. And they are great from an execution standpoint. Effective execution allows them to continually cut prices. They have some of the most sophisticated supply chain technology that you're going to find. They are excellent at what they see as their mission, which is written on their signs, "We sell for less."

On the other hand, they seem to have become despised by two important groups: a hard core group of their employees and many of the communities where they want to do business. I know that here in Denver they've been trying to build a Walmart store and there has been a lot of local opposition to it. That also seems to be the case in many other communities where they try to place a store.

This indicates that they have missed the boat on commitment and relationships. They have a lot of employees who aren't happy with them—much of that goes back to their part-time wages, their low pay, and probably more important, the fact that they don't provide healthcare coverage for the people who work for them. On the other hand, Walmart doesn't seem to be very good at building relationships in the communities where they want to do business.

I find Walmart to be an interesting dichotomy. They are so good at clarity and execution and so bad at commitment and relationships.

But to come back to relationships, relationships are not just about communities—relationships have to do with building strong partnerships with customers, suppliers, government regulators, your investors, as well as the communities where you do business.

Wright

Tell us about the book you're working on called *Star Power.*

Bilanich

It will be my fifth book. It comes from my work with individuals on how to become stars in their careers. It focuses on the five elements I mentioned previously: self-confidence, personal impact, performance, communication skills, and interpersonal competence.

As with most of my books, there will be several anecdotes and stories that I have personally experienced or that other people have shared with me. People can expect to see a good number of interesting and motivational quotes from a variety of people they know, and maybe from some people they don't know. The book ties to the Star Power work I do in coaching and in a new keynote speech I'm offering my audiences.

Wright

What a great conversation. I've taken copious notes here. I run a couple of companies and this information is very helpful and boy, have I been writing!

Today we have been talking with Bud Bilanich. His work focuses on improving the performance of individuals, teams, and entire organizations. If you've been reading this, I know you've gotten as much out of it as I have.

Bud, thank you so much for being with us today on *Speaking of Success.*

Bilanich

David, it's been my pleasure. Thanks for asking such great questions.

About the Author

Bud Bilanich's pragmatic approach to business, life, and the business of life has earned him the title The Common Sense Guy and made him one of the most sought after speakers, consultants, and executive coaches in the USA! Dr. Bilanich's work focuses on improving the performance of individuals, teams, and entire organizations. Bud is Harvard educated, but has a no-nonsense, commonsense approach to his work that stretches back to his roots in the steel country of Western Pennsylvania. His consulting and coaching clients report that he is full of practical, useful commonsense advice that they can put to work immediately. Audiences leave his Common Sense Keynotes armed with fundamentally sound, commonsense ideas and the motivation to put those ideas to work. Bud has thirty years of experience in the organization effectiveness field. He has worked with clients in the U.S., Canada, Latin America, Europe, Australia, and Asia. His clients include Pfizer Inc, Johnson & Johnson, Abbott Laboratories, Schein Pharmaceuticals, General Motors, Citicorp, JP Morgan Chase, AT&T, Pitney Bowes, Dana Corporation, and The Boys and Girls Clubs of America.

He is the author of six books: Fixing Performance Problems: Common Sense Ideas That Work, Four Secrets of High Performing Organizations, Leading With Values, Using Values To Turn Vision Into Reality, Solving Performance Problems: A Common Sense Guide for Leaders at all Levels, and Supervisory Leadership. Bud is a prolific writer. You can find his thoughts on contemporary business topics and issues on his popular blog: www.commonsenseguy.com. You can find more information on his work at his Web site: www.BudBilanich.com. Dr. Bilanich received an EdD from Harvard University with a concentration in Organizational Behavior and Intervention. He also holds an MA in Organizational and Interpersonal Communication from the University of Colorado, and a BS in Human Development from Penn State. Bud is a cancer survivor and lives in Denver, Colorado, with Cathy, his wife. He is a retired rugby player, an avid cyclist, and a film, live theatre, and crime fiction buff.

Bud Bilanich

The Common Sense Guy

875 South Colorado Boulevard, Suite 773

Denver, CO 80246

Phone: 303.393.0446

E-mail: Bud@BudBilanich.com

www.BudBilanich.com

Blog: www.CommonSenseGuy.com, Blog: www.CareerSuperStar.com

Chapter 8

BRIAN TRACY

THE INTERVIEW

David Wright (Wright)

Many years ago, Brian Tracy started off on a lifelong search for the secrets of success in life and business. He studied, researched, traveled, worked, and taught for more than thirty years. In 1981, he began to share his discoveries in talks and seminars, and eventually in books, audios and video-based courses.

The greatest secret of success he learned is this: "There are no secrets of success." There are instead timeless truths and principles that have to be rediscovered, relearned, and practiced by each person. Brian's gift is synthesis—the ability to take large numbers of ideas from many sources and combine them into highly practical, enjoyable, and immediately usable forms that people can take and apply quickly to improve their life and work. Brian has brought together the best ideas, methods, and techniques from thousands of books, hundreds of courses, and experience working with individuals and organizations of every kind in the U.S., Canada, and worldwide.

Today, I have asked Brian to discuss his latest book, *Victory!: Applying the Military Principals of Strategy for Success in Business and Personal Life.*

Brian Tracy, welcome to *Speaking of Success!*

Tracy

Thank you, David. It's a pleasure to be here.

Wright

Let's talk about your new book the *Victory! Applying* the *Military Principals* of *Strategy* for *Success* in *Business* and *Personal Life*. (By the way it is refreshing to hear someone say something good about the successes of the military.) Why do you think the military is so successful?

Tracy

Well, the military is based on very serious thought. The American military is the most respected institution in America. Unless you're a left liberal limp-wristed pinko most people in America really respect the military because it keeps America free. People who join the military give up most of their lives—twenty to thirty years—in sacrifice to be prepared to guard our freedoms. And if you ask around the world what it is that America stands for, it stands for individual freedom, liberty, democracy, freedom, and opportunity that is only secured in a challenging world—a dangerous world—by your military.

Now the other thing is, the people in our military are not perfect because there is no human institution made up of human beings that is perfect—there are no perfect people. The cost of mistakes in military terms is death; therefore, people in the military are extraordinarily serious about what they do. They are constantly looking for ways to do what they do better and better and better to reduce the likelihood of losing a single person.

We in America place extraordinary value on individual human life. That is why you will see millions of dollars spent to save a life, whether for an accident victim or Siamese twins from South America, because that's part of our culture. The military has that same culture.

I was just reading today about the RQ-1 "Predator" drone planes (Unmanned Aerial Vehicles—UAVs) that have been used in reconnaissance over the no-fly zones in Iraq. These planes fly back and forth constantly gathering information from the ground. They can also carry remote-controlled weapons. According to www.globalsecurity.org, the planes cost $4.5 million each and get shot down on a regular basis. However, the military is willing to invest hundreds of millions of dollars to develop these planes, and lose them to save the life of a pilot, because pilots are so precious—human life is precious. In the military everything is calculated right down to the tinniest detail because it's the smallest details that can cost lives. That is why the military is so successful—they are so meticulous about planning.

A salesperson can go out and make a call; if it doesn't work that's fine—he or she can make another sales call. Professional soldiers can go out on an operation and if it's not successful they're dead and maybe everybody in the squad is dead as well. There is no margin for error in the military; that's why they do it so well. This is also why the military principals of strategy that I talk about in *Victory!* are so incredibly important because a person who really understands those principals and strategies sees how to do things vastly better with far lower probability of failure than the average person.

Wright

In the promotion on *Victory!* you affirm that it is very important to set clear attainable goals and objectives. Does that theme carry out through all of your presentations and all of your books?

Tracy

Yes. Over and over again the theme reiterates that you can't hit a target you can't see—you shouldn't get into your car unless you know where you are going. More people spend more time planning a picnic than they spend planning their careers.

I'll give you an example. A very successful woman who is in her fifties now wrote down a plan when she was attending university. Her plan was for the first ten years she would work for a Fortune 500 corporation, really learn the business, and learn how to function at high levels. For the second ten years of her career she talked about getting married and having children at the same time. For that second ten years she would also work for a medium sized company helping it grow and succeed. For the third ten years (between the ages of forty and fifty), she would start her own company based on her knowledge of both businesses. She would then build that into a successful company. Her last ten years she would be chief executive officer of a major corporation and retire financially independent at the age of sixty. At age fifty-eight she would have hit every single target. People would say, "Boy, you sure are lucky." No, it wouldn't be luck. From the time she was seventeen she was absolutely crystal clear about what she was going to do with her career and what she was going to do with her life, and she hit all of her targets.

Wright

In a time where companies, both large and small, take a look at their competition and basically try to copy everything they do, it was really interesting to read in *Victory!* that you suggest taking vigorous offensive action to get the best results. What do you mean by "vigorous offensive action"?

Tracy

Well, see, that's another thing. When you come back to talking about probabilities—and this is really important—you see successful people try more things. And if you wanted to just end the interview right now and ask, "What piece of advice would you give to our listeners?" I would say, "Try more things." The reason I would say that is because if you try more things, the probability is that you will hit your target.

For example, here's an analogy I use. Imagine that you go into a room and there is a dartboard against the far wall. Now imagine that you are drunk and you have never played darts before. The room is not very bright and you can barely see the bull's eye. You are standing along way from the board, but you have an endless supply of darts. You pick up the darts and you just keep throwing them at the target over there on the other of the room even though you are not a good dart thrower and you're not even well coordinated. If you kept throwing darts over and over again what would you eventually hit?

Wright

Pretty soon you would get a bulls eye.

Tracy

Yes, eventually you would hit a bull's eye. The odds are that as you keep throwing the darts even though you are not that well educated, even if you don't come from a wealthy family or you don't have a Harvard education, if you just keep throwing darts you will get a little better each time you throw. It's known as a "decybernetic self-correction mechanism" in the brain—each time you try something, you get a little bit smarter at it. So over time, if you kept throwing, you must eventually hit a bull's eye. In other words, you must eventually find the right way to do the things you need to do to become a millionaire. That's the secret of success. That's why people come here from a 190 countries with one idea in mind—"If I come here I can try anything I want; I can go anywhere, because there are no limitations. I have so much freedom; and if I keep doing this, then by God, I will eventually hit a bulls eye." And they do and everybody says, "Boy, you sure where lucky."

Now imagine another scenario: You are thoroughly trained at throwing darts—you have practiced, you have developed skills and expertise in your field, you are constantly upgrading your knowledge, and you practice all the time. Second you are completely prepared, you're thoroughly cold sober, fresh, fit, alert, with high energy. Third, all of the room is very bright around the dartboard. This time how long would it take you to hit the bull's eye? The obvious answer is you will hit a bull's eye far faster than if you had all those negative conditions.

What I am I saying is, you can dramatically increase the speed at which you hit your bull's eye. The first person that I described—drunk, unprepared, in a darkened room, and so on may take twenty or twenty-five years. But if you are thoroughly prepared, constantly upgrading your skills; if you are very clear about your targets; if you have everything you need at hand and your target is clear, your chances of hitting a bull's eye you could hit a bull's eye is five years rather than twenty. That's the difference in success in life.

Wright

In reading your books and watching your presentations on video, one of the common threads seen through your presentations is creativity. I was glad that in the promotional material of *Victory!* you state that you need to apply innovative solutions to overcome obstacles. The word "innovative" grabbed me. I guess you are really concerned with *how* people solve problems rather than just solving problems.

Tracy

Vigorous action means you will cover more ground. What I say to people, especially in business, is the more things you do the more experience you get. The more experience you get the smarter you get. The smarter you get the better results you get the better results you get. The better results you get the less time it takes you to get the same results. And it's such a simple thing. In my books *Create Your Own Future* and *Victory!* you will find there is one characteristic of all successful people—they are action oriented. They move fast, they move quickly, and they don't waste time. They're moving ahead, trying more things, but they are always in motion. The faster you move the more energy you have. The faster you move the more in control you feel and the faster you are the more positive and the more motivated you are. We are talking about a direct relationship between vigorous action and success.

Wright

Well, the military certainly is a team "sport" and you talk about building peak performance teams for maximum results. My question is how do individuals in corporations build peak performance teams in this culture?

Tracy

One of the things we teach is the importance of selecting people carefully. Really successful companies spend an enormous amount of time at the front end on selection they look for people who are really, really good in terms of what they are looking for. They interview very carefully; they interview several people and they interview them several times. They do careful background checks. They are as careful in selecting people as a person might be in getting married. Again, in the military, before a person is promoted they go through a rigorous process. In large corporations, before a person is promoted his or her performance is very, very carefully evaluated to be sure they are the right people to be promoted at that time.

Wright

My favorite point in *Victory!* is when you say, "Amaze your competitors with surprise and speed." I have done that several times in business and it does work like a charm.

Tracy

Yes, it does. Again one of the things we teach over and over again that there is a direct relationship between speed and perceived value. When you do things fast for people they consider you to be better. They consider your products to be better and they consider your service to be better—they actually consider them to be of higher value. Therefore, if you do things really, really fast then you overcome an enormous amount of resistance. People wonder, "Is this a good decision? Is it worth the money? Am I going the right direction?" When you do things fast, you blast that out of their minds.

Wright

You talk about moving quickly to seize opportunities. I have found that to be difficult. When I ask people about opportunities, it's difficult to find out what they think an opportunity is. Many think opportunities are high-risk, although I've never found it that way myself. What do you mean by moving quickly to cease opportunity?

Tracy

There are many cases were a person has an idea and they think that's a good idea. They think they should do something about it. They think, "I am going to do something about that but I really can't do it this week, so I will wait till after the month ends," and so on. By the time they do move on the opportunity it's to late—somebody's already seized it.

One of the military examples I use is the battle of Gettysburg. Now the battle of Gettysburg was considered the high-water mark of the Confederacy after the battle of Gettysburg the Confederacy won additional battles at Chattanooga and other places but they eventually lost the war. The high-water mark of Gettysburg was a little hill at one end of the battlefield called Little Round Top. As the battle began Little Round Top was empty. Colonel Joshua Chamberlain of the Union Army saw that this could be the pivotal point of the battlefield. He went up there and looked at it and he immediately rushed troops to fortify the hill. Meanwhile, the Confederates also saw that Little Round Top could be key to the battle as well, so they too immediately rushed the hill. An enormous battle took place. It was really the essence of the battle of Gettysburg. The victor who took that height controlled the battlefield. Eventually the union troops, who were almost lost, controlled Little Round Top and won the battle. The Civil War was over in about a year and a half, but that was the turning point.

So what would have happened if Chamberlain had said, "Wait until after lunch and then I'll move some men up to Little Round Top"? The Confederate troops would have seized Little Round Top, controlled the battlefield, and would have won the battle of Gettysburg. It was just a matter of moving very, very fast. Forty years later it was determined that there were three days at the battle of Gettysburg that cost the battle for the Confederates. The general in charge of the troops on the Confederate right flank was General James Longstreet. Lee told him to move his army forward as quickly as possible the next day, but to use his own judgment. Longstreet didn't agree with Lee's plan so he kept his troop sitting there most of the next day. It is said that it was Longstreet's failure to move forward on the second day and seize Little Round Top that cost the Confederacy the battle and eventually the war. It was just this failure to move forward and forty years later, when Longstreet appeared at a reunion of Confederate veterans in 1901 or 1904, he was booed. The veterans felt his failure to move forward that fateful day cost them the war. If you read every single account of the battle of Gettysburg, Longstreet's failure to move forward and quickly seize the opportunity is always included.

Wright

In your book you tell your readers to get the ideas and information needed to succeed. Where can individuals get these ideas?

Tracy

Well we are living in an ocean of ideas. It's so easy. The very first thing you do is you pick a subject you want to major in and you go to someone who is good at it. You ask what you should read in this field and you go down to the bookstore and you look at the books. Any book that is published in paperback obviously sold well in hardcover. Read the table of contents. Make sure the writer has experience in the area you in which you want to learn about. Buy the book and read it. People ask, "How can I be sure it is the right book?" You can't be sure; stop trying to be sure.

When I go to the bookstore I buy three or four books and bring them home and read them. I may only find one chapter of a book that's helpful, but that chapter may save me a year of hard work.

The fact is that your life is precious. A book costs twenty of thirty dollars. How much is your life worth? How much do you earn per hour? A person who earns fifty thousand dollars a year earns twenty-five dollars an hour. A person who wants to earn a hundred thousand dollars a year earns fifty dollars an hour. Now, if a book cost you ten or twenty dollars but it can save you a year of hard work, then that's the cheapest thing you have bought in your whole life. And what if you bought fifty books and you paid twenty dollars apiece for them—a thousand dollars worth of books—and out of that you only got one idea that saved you a year of hard work? You've got a fifty times payoff. So the rule is you cannot prepare too thoroughly.

Wright

In the last several months I have recommended your book, *Get Paid More and Promoted Faster* to more people. I have had a lot of friends in their fifties and sixties who have lost their jobs to layoffs all kinds of transfers of ownership. When I talked with you last, the current economy had a 65 percent jump in layoffs. In the last few months before I talked with you, every one of them reported that the book really did help them. They saw some things a little bit clearer; it was a great book.

How do you turn setbacks and difficulties to your advantage? I know what it means, but what's the process?

Tracy

You look into it you look into every setback and problem and find the seed of an equal or greater advantage or benefit. It's a basic rule. You find that all successful people look into their problems for lessons they can learn and for things they can turn to their advantage. In fact, one of the best attitudes you can possibly have is to say that you know every problem that is sent to you is sent to help you. So your job is just simply look into to it and ask, "What can help me in this situation?" And surprise, surprise! You will find something that can help you. You will find lessons you can learn; you will find something you can do more of, or less of; you can find something that will give you an insight that will set you in a different direction, and so on.

Wright

I am curious. I know you have written a lot in the past and you are a terrific writer. Your cassette programs are wonderful. What do you have planned for the next few years?

Tracy

Aside from speaking and consulting with non-profits, my goal is to produce four books a year on four different subjects, all of which have practical application to help people become more successful.

Wright

Well, I really want to thank you for your time here today on *Speaking of Success!* It's always fascinating to hear what you have to say. I know I have been a Brian Tracy fan for many, many years. I really appreciate your being with us today.

Tracy

Thank you. You have a wonderful day and I hope our listeners and readers will go out and get *Focal Point* and/or *Victory!* They are available at any bookstore or at Amazon.com. They are fabulous books, filled with good ideas that will save you years of hard work.

Wright

I have already figured out that those last two books are a better buy with Amazon.com, so you should go to your computer and buy these books as soon as possible.

We have been talking today with Brian Tracy, whose life and career truly makes one of the best rags-to-riches stories. Brian didn't graduate from high school and his first job was washing dishes. He lost job after job—washing cars, pumping gas, stacking lumber, you name it. He was homeless and living in his car. Finally, he got into sales, then sales management. Later, he sold investments, developed real estate, imported and distributed Japanese automobiles, and got a master's degree in business administration. Ultimately, he became the COO of a $265 million dollar development company.

Brian, you are quite a person. Thank you so much for being with us today.

Tracy

You are very welcome, David. You have a great day!

About The Author

One of the world's top success motivational speakers, Brian Tracy is the author of may books and audio tape seminars, including *The Psychology of Achievement, The Luck Factor, Breaking the Success Barrier, Thinking Big* and *Success Is a Journey.*

Brian Tracy
www.BrianTracy.com

Chapter 9

KATHLYNN MCCONNELL

THE INTERVIEW

David Wright (Wright)

Today we're talking with Kathlynn McConnell. She is founder and president of Lifestyle Consulting Services. She is a "professional refueler," energizing individuals and organizations for enhanced peak performance both personally and professionally. She speaks to thousands of people each year, encouraging them to cultivate healthy relationships with co-workers, uncover values in the workplace and in life, reduce stress, balance priorities, refuel, find meaning in their work, and so much more. Front line associates as well as CEOs value the passionate and purposeful information she brings to light. Kathlynn is a member of the International Speakers Network, National Speakers Association, American Society for Training and Development, Chamber of Commerce, and Vice President of the Professional Women's Network.

Kathlynn, welcome to *Speaking of Success.*

Kathlynn McConnell (McConnell)

Thank you.

Wright

So tell me, how did you choose to start your own business?

McConnell

Never in my wildest dreams while growing up did I ever consider owning my own business. I was born without that business sense gene. I always wanted to be a teacher. My mother would catch me using my bedroom wall for a chalkboard while I was teaching my stuffed animal "students."

The idea of opening my own business didn't occur to me until our second child was born. Kale arrived two months early while we were vacationing out of town—talk about timing! We were told he had a fifty-fifty chance of survival as the doctors were putting him on a Life-flight helicopter to take him to a larger city where they had a neonatal intensive care unit. His lungs weren't fully developed, he had a hole in his heart, he didn't have a swallow reflex, and he had severely crossed eyes. Later we discovered he also had a muscle disease that affected his movements.

He spent almost two months in the neonatal intensive care unit. Upon release he required physical therapy at least four times a week, leg braces, numerous eye surgeries, and constant appointments with various doctors along the way.

That was a tough schedule to have and hold down a daytime job at the same time. My husband and I decided I would find a job at night so I could take care of our son's special needs as well as our four-year-old daughter during the day. Then we would switch roles at the front door and my husband would take care of them at night when I went off to work at the local grocery store to bag groceries as I envisioned my college diploma getting dusty on my desk at home.

While I was packing groceries at ten o'clock on a Friday night, I thought, "There has got to be a different way to utilize the skills I developed in college." As I was carefully placing a carton of eggs in a customer's bag I happened to discover that this particular customer worked at a private university and they were searching for an evening class instructor in one of their new programs. To my delight, this program just happened to align with my degree. The next day I went down to the university, applied, and got the teaching job.

Teaching at night still allowed our family the flexibility and income we needed at the time. That's when it really struck me—I had become the teacher I had always wanted to be. I had a passion for encouraging individuals, not only to discover their potential but also to find out how best to use it.

I was still searching for that balance in my life, however. I loved the teaching but the hours were very difficult. I was up at 4:30 every morning getting our daughter ready for school, our son to his numerous doctor appointments, and putting together lesson plans. After supper I'd rush off to teach until ten at night, come home, correct papers, go to bed after midnight, then get up and start all over again.

After a year I reevaluated the situation. That's when my husband finally said to me, "Why don't you do this on your own?"

"What! Start a school?" I asked. "Are you crazy?"

"No," he said. "Start a business where you can inspire people. You can still teach and help them uncover their talents so they can reach their peak performance in the workplace as well as in the rest of their life. Not only could you still serve others with your passion, you could also have a little more control over the hours that you put into each day and find a balance between work and life."

That's when the idea of Lifestyle Consulting Services began. As the children grew, so did the business.

Wright

With two small children and overwhelming medical bills to deal with, how supportive were your family and friends of your new venture?

McConnell

My father thought I was nuts! He was a statistician by trade—not much of a risk-taker. He had the same job for most of his life so he thought I was jumping off the deep end. He thought that packing groceries was a very secure job—people will always have to eat, therefore I would always have groceries to pack! Some of my extended relatives agreed with my dad. But my husband was my true cheerleader. He saw the potential in me that I didn't even realize was there. He encouraged me to focus on my principles, follow my heart, contribute with the gifts and talents I'd been given, and to find the joy that comes with serving with your whole self.

Wright

Without prior experience, how difficult was it for you to make contacts and build up your business? Where did you start?

McConnell

Remember, I didn't have that business sense gene so I needed help! Following your dream isn't always as easy a journey as one might think. I loved the development of the programs, the presenting, interacting, meeting people, and making a difference—that's my passion. But a business does not run on passion alone, as I found out. So I sought out a small business development center to guide me through the business and marketing plan, and financial record keeping—those pesky little details that are necessary to succeed but certainly weren't in my area of interest or strength.

I secured interviews with consultants and speakers in the business to gather some background information and knowledge, and learn from the paths they took on their journey to success. The first gentleman I interviewed listened patiently to my ideas of starting my own company. Then he leaned forward, gently patted my hand, and told me, "That's a nice dream, but I just don't think you have it in you to be successful in the business world. I think it would be best if you just worked for someone else." I think of him every time I go to the bank to deposit a check from a client . . . and I smile.

I have also joined organizations that would help me not only meet individuals in the industry but also educate me along the way such as The American Society for Training and Development, International Speakers Network, National Speakers Association, Chamber of Commerce, and numerous networking groups.

Wright

What's your definition of success?

McConnell

Ahh, the sweet sound of success! That sound is different for everyone. Although money is definitely necessary to support your life, your family, and your dreams, I believe true success is measured more in serving others and principles rather than merely dollar signs. Principles are the core of who you are and if that core is based on respect, joy, peace, patience, kindness, goodness, faithfulness, gentleness, and self-control *and* you have the courage to live them and balance them in your life, *that's* success.

Wright

You define yourself as a "professional refueler." Will you tell me more about what that means?

McConnell

Well, David, I bet you drive your car often, right? I daresay you've had to fill the gas tank on a regular basis. What happens to the car when the gas tank reaches empty?

Wright

Basically, it stops!

McConnell

Exactly. The car quits moving forward. It doesn't matter whether you have a beautiful Mercedes or a dandy Dodge, you cannot reach your desired destination if you are running on empty. So that's where I come in—I give you a little "gasoline" so to speak. I help individuals remember how to be human *beings* while they're human doings. I inspire individuals to uncover who they really are—what their talents and values and passions are—so they can make their own unique contributions in the world of work as well as in their personal life.

I encourage organizations and individuals to define their own meaning of success and support them on their journey. I *refuel* organizations and individuals.

Wright

As you plan your presentations, how do you choose the topics?

McConnell

That's a good question. I have had the privilege of working with organizations as small as little two-employee coffee shops to as large as world renowned medical care facilities. These diverse businesses all have one thing in common: they employ and serve people from all walks of life. I listen to the life stories of the business owners, managers, and associates alike. I ask what their struggles are and what they think they need to move forward and be successful.

Inevitably the needs are the same, no matter how big or small the organization is or what the title of the individual within the organization is. Owners and managers want to know how to help their associates discover strengths, manage their emotions, get motivated, communicate with each other, and enjoy what they do. I turn that information into presentations.

Wright

What would you say have been the biggest obstacles you have faced in your successful journey?

McConnell

There are two of them that I still struggle with today: fear of the "what ifs" and the gremlins—those little but very powerful negative thoughts that cause self-doubt and focus on failure. So often our gremlins keep us paralyzed by past mistakes that we talk ourselves right out of any movement forward or hope for success.

I keep these two obstacles at bay by arming myself with positive, supportive people. I work hard to stay healthy mentally and physically. I work with several life coaches who touch base with me every now and then and help me turn fears and self-doubts into effective energy that moves me forward into the future while I'm enjoying the present and learning from the past.

Wright

Many years ago a brilliant man told me that if I am walking down the road and come to a fence post with a turtle sitting on top of it that I could bet he didn't get up there by himself. Who do you keep close in your circle of influence and why?

McConnell

I am so blessed to have a wide variety of individuals in my circle of influence. The people I interact with range from CEOs to those who are homeless because I can learn many life lessons from everyone I encounter. It's my hope that I can support and give back to those people as well.

The individuals I choose to keep closest to me are those who not only support me but who challenge me to take that next step. I look for mentors who do that. I look for joyful people—optimists—individuals who are problem solvers not problem seekers. I associate with many diverse kinds of people. Not everybody has the same opinion as I do but that's where the growth comes from.

Wright

Will you tell me why an organization would hire someone like you—a professional refueler?

McConnell

It's difficult to quantify in numbers what I do but wise organizations get past that. They realize that no matter how fabulous their new and improved product is or how advanced their technology has become, their bottom line truly is dependent on the people who sell that new improved product or push the buttons on the advanced technical devices. The organizations that understand this are willing to invest in their most important assets—their associates.

I encourage and help individuals and organizations to strive to reach their full potential, to cultivate healthy relationships with coworkers, and uncover values in the workplace and in life, to reduce stress, and balance those priorities so they can be successful personally and professionally. When people have a greater sense of well being and discover their strengths and talents, they tend to step out of their comfort zones more often and go to the next level with a greater sense of confidence and commitment. They *as well as* their organizations benefit.

Wright

As a professional refueler, do you ever need to be refueled yourself?

McConnell

Oh yes, definitely! Owning a business is a commitment; it can be very consuming and can suck you dry if you don't pay attention. For instance, just for a moment think of a pitcher of water and several empty glasses on a table. If I continually fill up everyone else's glass but never stop to refuel my pitcher, then I'm the one who becomes empty and I'm unable to continue to help anyone else.

I think it's extremely important to pay attention to the things that lift my spirits, relax me, enhance my knowledge, and bring me joy so that I don't end up empty. I have posted a phrase on my computer screen, "Never get too busy making a living that you forget to make a life," to remind me to refuel myself. I have to live what I preach or my words are empty to others.

Wright

After more than twelve years in the business, do you ever get nervous before you speak to a group?

McConnell

I have a herd of butterflies in my stomach that take flight before every presentation, whether it's a crowd of two thousand or ten. I can feel my hands start to get a little clammy and my throat tenses up. But I welcome that adrenalin and the nerves because they remind me not to take any of this for granted. Every time I'm speaking to a group I have the privilege of sharing information that will make a difference to someone in need. I want to make a contribution that is meaningful. I never want to get complacent. I take my mission of making a difference very seriously.

Wright

What are some of the most important life lessons you have gained from your journey?

McConnell

My life journey has taught me so many lessons. One comes from a very wise man who happens to be my husband. Remember him—my cheerleader? He constantly reminds me of the fact that a situation is what it is. And wishing it were otherwise won't change it. With that in mind, the life lesson is to grab hold of what I *can* do with what is rather than waste time lamenting on what isn't and what I don't have.

Another life lesson came from one of my college professors. He told me that if it is to be, it's up to me. This means that no one else is going to do it for me. Everyone has the power of potential but success comes from putting that potential into action.

One of my favorite life lessons is described by a quote from Freya Stark, French adventurer and explorer, who said, "There can be no happiness if the things we believe in are different from the things we do." We all have values but we don't often take time to make them priorities in our life. Each day I remind myself of what is important, to live in the moment, not to get stuck by the events that happened in the past or fear the unknown of the future, but be aware of my values in *this* season of life and to serve those around me.

Today really is a gift and that's why it's called the present, so unwrap the gift of the present.

Wright

What an interesting conversation. I really appreciate your taking all this time with me to answer these questions. I've learned a lot and I know our readers will.

McConnell

Excellent! Well, my mission for today is complete then.

Wright

Today we have been talking with Kathlynn McConnell, president of Lifestyle Consulting Services. She speaks to thousands of people each year, encouraging them to cultivate healthy relationships with coworkers, uncover values in the workplace and in life, reduce stress, balance priorities, and basically refuel and find meaning in their work and life. She speaks to frontline associates as well as to CEOs in almost every conceivable condition.

I don't know about you but after this conversation today, I think she knows what she's talking about.

Kathlynn, thank you so much for being with us on *Speaking of Success.*

About the Author

Kathlynn McConnell, president of Lifestyle Consulting Services, is a Professional Refueler, bringing energy to the programs she gives and encouragement to the people she serves. She draws from her experiences as a professional, a teacher, business owner, wife, mother, and race car driver to inspire individuals to cultivate healthy relationships and improve business communications, uncover values in the workplace and life, reduce stress, balance priorities, refuel, and make a life . . . not just a living.

Kathlynn McConnell
Lifestyle Consulting Services
4612 Glenwood Street
Duluth, MN 55804
Phone: 218.390.0515
E-mail: livingpotential@aol.com
www.refuelinglives.com

Chapter 10

ROBERT BERKLEY

THE INTERVIEW

David Wright (Wright)

Today we are speaking with Rob Berkley, an acclaimed Master Certified Coach, best known for his ability to transform businesses and lives as an executive coach and business advisor. For nearly two decades prior to his present undertaking, he's been an entrepreneur and an executive for such organizations as Bankers' Trust, Simon & Schuster, and Pearson. Pearson is one of the world's largest media organizations. Today, he coaches Fortune 500 senior executives, entrepreneurs, and professionals. He also co-developed Vision Day®, a customized, strategic planning session that helps people craft and fulfill inspiring personal and career visions.

Rob's clients describe him as a blend of Yoda, Gandhi, and Perry Mason, combining wisdom, clarity, kindness, and a touch of "The Force." He lives and works with his partner, Debbie Phillips, on Martha's Vineyard, Massachusetts, and Naples, Florida, where they hold Vision Day workshops and retreats. Today Rob will tell us about Vision Day and how to increase your success, your fulfillment, and your peace of mind by holding your own personal, strategic planning day.

Rob, welcome to *Speaking of Success.*

Rob Berkley (Berkley)
Thank you, David.

Wright
So, tell me, how do you define success?

Berkley
A successful person is someone who is doing what they love well. People who are successful feel connected to their purpose in life and can point to the ways they are expressing that purpose. Success goes beyond status, although successful people are often well recognized for the value they create. Success goes beyond money, even though successful people usually have enough money to rise above life's struggles.

In our business, we sometimes see "successful" people who don't love what they do and aren't fulfilled by it, even though they may achieve considerable status and financial rewards. But they're not successful in their own minds.

Life for successful people is not always in perfect balance and there can be bad days of course, but overall successful people are joyful, engaged, and fulfilled. They do not want for the essentials necessary to living a good life.

Wright
If you had to pick just one approach to help people become more successful, what would that approach be?

Berkley
I would urge people to take at least one completely uninterrupted day every year out of their complex lives to plan that year and decide what they would like to have in the next twelve or so months of their life. In our coaching practice we created Vision Day, a personalized, strategic planning day for this very purpose.

Wright
That concept certainly seems like a logical and beneficial idea. So why wouldn't someone who wants success jump right on this idea? It's only one or two days out of the entire year. That's not much time to spend to plan on how to achieve what you want.

Berkley

The huge personal and professional demands put on busy people today often stand in the way of thinking about their own dreams and goals. So time dedicated solely to themselves is often delayed, postponed, or thought of as something to do somewhere off in the future.

You know who's brilliant at this concept? Bill Gates. Once or twice a year he has "Think Week" where he closets himself alone in a cottage in upstate Washington. No phone calls or e-mails. There he reads and relaxes for a week. He has linked many great Microsoft initiatives directly to the time spent during his unencumbered week.

Although our clients usually devote an abundance of resources, talent, and personal commitment to success, what they often lack is the most precious commodity of all—time. We've seen over and over that time spent on Vision Day—or on personal, strategic planning—is an investment that pays huge dividends, personally and professionally.

Wright

Expand on that idea a bit if you would.

Berkley

After a Vision Day, we've seen people write books, change careers, start businesses, sell businesses, take their businesses to new levels, find the relationship of their dreams, start foundations, take dream vacations, invent new products and services, retire (or unretire for that matter), and achieve many other remarkable, exciting goals!

In addition, these folks receive that unquantifiable dividend of feeling greater satisfaction and fulfillment because they've chosen to live life closer to their true dreams and desires.

Wright

What situations do you find Vision Day the most helpful for?

Berkley

Vision Day is beneficial for four critical and yet quite different situations.

The first is when someone is going through a major life change or professional transition. It can be a planned transition such as a promotion or retirement or quitting a job and taking a new one. Or, that change can be an unplanned transition such as losing a job or facing a loss, a divorce, illness, or the death of a loved one.

The second kind of Vision Day is for someone with a big dream that he or she wants to share with the world. That "vision" can be taking a company—or a passion—to the next level of achievement or growth.

For instance, a veteran of five Vision Days, Laurie Forster of Easton, Maryland, took her love and expert knowledge of wine to become "America's premier wine coach." Her mission is to connect people to each other through wine education, wine-tasting events, and trips that help "spirit away" the snootiness often associated with drinking wine. Her tagline, which I love, is: "De-mystifying wine, one glass at a time!"

A third situation is that person who at some level needs to shake life up a bit to figure out what comes next.

Nancy Neal, a very successful eating disorder counselor in Greenville, South Carolina, is a great example of this situation. With her Vision Day plan in hand, she took a year's sabbatical and explored her many other passions and interests. Only months into it, she became the co-host of a television show about nature. It was a totally unexpected move but it deeply fulfilled her core value and passion for nature!

A fourth use is for someone who simply wants to have a great year. After years of dedication and noted success in software sales, executive Allison Barry spent more than a year planning her next steps and "great year." Currently enjoying the plan, she "retired" from her job, moved to Boston, and vacationed in France. She took classes in subjects she loved, but never had time for, and became a "mini-Oprah" when she set up a surprise for her parents, fulfilling their long-held dream of meeting former President Bill Clinton.

Wright

Can everybody benefit from a Vision Day?

Berkley

David, I just realized I used all women as examples of the purposes for Vision Day. So to begin answering your question, we have equal numbers of men and women participating in Vision Day.

The process works for anyone who is willing and open to creating a great life. We've had everyone from corporate CEOs to full-time parents, as well as physicians and politicians. We've hosted entrepreneurs, hospital administrators, senior-level executives, lawyers, coaches, chefs, journalists, filmmakers, authors, musicians, and healers. The chief characteristic of a person who can benefit is someone who wants more out of life. They value themselves and see themselves as part of an ongoing creative process. And of course they love improving on life. One of the things that is most gratifying to us are the rare people who say that they don't think Vision Day will work for them but who are open to trying it anyway. To their pleasant surprise, the results they get are very useful.

On the other hand, there are some people that Vision Day won't work for. These are people who are set in their ways. They're satisfied or "married" to their present way of doing things and believe that's good enough. They have no need and no desire for increased fulfillment or joy or health or income. These are people who want someone else to fix what's wrong in their lives. They are hoping someone will simply give them the answer.

Vision Day, of course, is about each person discovering his or her own answers, not us giving answers to them.

Wright

How does a person prepare for Vision Day? Is there some follow-up afterward?

Berkley

Leading up to Vision Day, we spend time preparing with you to make sure you are clear about what you want to get out of your day. We ask you to participate in thought-provoking exercises to determine what it is you really want. Sometimes we even ask you to write your life story. Then, you're ready to visit Martha's Vineyard or Naples for your special day. Afterward, you receive a report from us with all the notes and goals that you compiled during your Vision Day.

Within a month, there is a follow-up coaching session to answer questions and keep you on track to reach your goals. For anyone who needs continued support, we offer ongoing coaching and consulting. We view ourselves as your partner, walking forward with you as you execute your Vision Day plan.

Wright

Rob, Vision Day is really intriguing as I learn more about the concept. Will you tell us some more stories about Vision Day and the results people have had?

Berkley

I thought you'd never ask! That's the most exciting part of Vision Day—the results that often come afterward. Sometimes I feel like a proud father and want to whip out my photograph album filled with all the Vision Day participants. I want to showcase their achievements and speak about all of their success! It is important to know, however, that most of the work we do is confidential and unless people explicitly give us permission to share their stories, we keep their privacy.

One of the stories I can speak about is Joe Caronna. Joe was working for a company that was going to be acquired by IBM. So, with a big career change looming, Joe came to Vision Day to create a success plan for his new position. As soon as his success plan for IBM was complete and he saw his path forward, Joe had a realization of the heart. I still remember the excitement on his face when that moment occurred.

Joe discovered that he had a powerful desire to make an important contribution to the world hemophilia community. Hemophilia is a congenital disorder that leads to uncontrolled bleeding and usually affects males. Joe's young son Alex has hemophilia, and although Joe and his family had been supported over the years by the existing hemophilia organization, Joe knew that the available services didn't go far enough.

There was no place in the community that focused exclusively on the educational and emotional needs of men who are affected by this disorder. So, during Joe's Vision Day he created a dual plan—one for his success as a manager at IBM and another to launch a nonprofit organization to provide education and hope for men and their families who are affected by bleeding disorders. The result was that five years later Joe is now a top manager at IBM and has launched a non-profit organization called Inalex Communications. Today, Inalex provides education, hope, and inspiration to thousands of men and their families in the hemophilia community.

Wright

I'm curious. Will you tell me about someone who invented a product or service after Vision Day?

Berkley

Oh, yes! Another powerful Vision Day success story is Christopher Celeste. When I first met Christopher, he was president of a successful technology marketing firm. Due to a change in his family situation he had moved to another city, which left him trying to figure out how to continue to pursue his career. Would he return to similar work? Would he become a consultant? Or would he do something totally new? These concerns weighed heavily on his mind during a *transition* type of Vision Day.

Christopher's revelation during Vision Day was that he wanted to create his own organization where he could bring something completely new to his life and do something different—something that hadn't existed before. So, he created a plan to work with partners, invent a new idea, and bring it to market. That idea now is framed by the Findaway Company where he and others invented a product called the "Playaway," the first self-playing, digital audio book where all you have to do is listen. It was less than two years from the inception of this idea to having the products in stores! You have probably seen the product. It is already in Borders and Barnes and Noble bookstores. Playaways are about the size of two matchboxes and contain an entire book. The product is absolutely fantastic and Christopher is now doing exactly what he set out to do on his Vision Day.

Wright

That's exciting! Anyone else's story you'd like to share?

Berkley

Another story that is particularly moving for Debbie and me is Maureen Riopelle. Shortly before Maureen came to her first Vision Day in October 2003, her mother died of cancer. She was a publishing executive and dreamed of starting a foundation to honor her mother, but wasn't sure of the focus. During her Vision Day, she created a plan for changing the work she was doing then and began mapping out and creating groundwork to start that foundation sometime in the future.

Shockingly, a few weeks after her Vision Day, Maureen's own world was turned upside down when she herself was diagnosed with breast cancer. As she neared the completion of her own extensive treatments, Maureen returned for her second Vision Day . . . I still get emotional when I talk about Maureen's experience.

This time the focus of her Vision Day was to craft a vision and plan with the critical next steps in developing her mother's namesake—The Mary Maguire Foundation. One of Maureen's strongest core values is her love for and desire to help other people. Her own cancer experience led her to identify a specific problem: a huge underserved population—the 10 million of cancer survivors who are unsure how to return to their "normal" lives after their cancer experience. There are surprisingly few services for these cancer survivors. Her mission now is to change that situation.

The Mary Maguire Foundation will hold its first retreat in October 2006 to support forty cancer survivors and help them create next steps and life plans and give them a sense of hope and healing and a future. Maureen's foundation is able to cover the entire cost of this weekend, and we think it will be a beautiful event. In three years, she has gone from a full-time job doing something she liked to full-time work doing what she believes she was put on this earth to accomplish. To meet Maureen is to be inspired!

Wright

Sounds fantastic and also rather humbling I think.

Berkley

I'd also like to tell you about Ray Sawyer. Ray was a very successful lawyer from Cleveland, facing retirement. He had had a long and illustrious career and at one point, he was even the chief of staff for the Governor of Ohio. Ray was too young to retire. He had a lot of energy and no intention of becoming a sedentary retiree.

The first thing he decided was that he no longer wanted to practice as a lawyer. But he was unsure of what he should do next. He needed an encore. In his favor, one of his personal gifts and talents was an extraordinary ability to connect people and ideas. He is a natural connector, the caliber of person you read about in Malcolm Gladwell's book, *The Tipping Point.*

What Ray discovered during Vision Day was that the second act of his life was waiting in the wings. Prior to that day, I don't think he ever imagined he could produce Broadway plays. Part of his Vision

Day plan, however, was to "taste and test" the New York world of theater. He joined the advisory council at the Julliard School where he began to meet fascinating people connected to Broadway. He used his incredible networking and connecting skills to talk to people about the possibilities for someone with his experience and abilities. The result was pretty phenomenal. Ray and his wife, Kit, ended up investing in and participating in the success of several productions. The Broadway shows, *Urinetown* and *Wicked*, are two of the many successes he has been involved in. And he's worked tirelessly behind the scenes to fund and connect countless people to pursue their own dreams in theater and the arts. Bravo, Ray!

Wright

So, what are some of the topics that must be included in a planning day like Vision Day?

Berkley

There are five aspects we feel are absolutely essential in a strategic planning day. First is to engage an experienced business advisor or coach. That person should be someone with great facilitation skills to guide you and is also someone you feel comfortable with. The person you choose should have comprehensive professional experience, training in the dynamics of personal facilitation, and expertise in adult education and how people change. There are many coaches and business advisors available today, so it is best to get a recommendation from others who have used their services and can vouch for their expertise and involvement.

Second, we highly recommend that the work should include an identification of your core values. Even if you think you know your values, we've learned there is an art and a specific science to discovering and clarifying those values, so it is to your benefit to have someone help you with that undertaking. It is very rare that we meet someone whose personal values are as clear to him or her as they could be.

Third, the facilitator should have the ability to help you identify blocks and any resistance to change that can stand in the way of your success. This component of a strategic planning day accelerates your ability to progress and achieve. There are some unique techniques Debbie and I use that make it much easier for people to identify and remove the blocks that hold them back.

Fourth is a reliable goal-setting process. Even though goal-setting is a popular topic these days, we still find that people lack clarity and don't often set good goals. It's been surprising in our work with executives to see how many don't have a tried-and-true method for setting goals. I would say that a large percentage of what holds people back is fuzziness about what they need and want in their lives.

Fifth is a mechanism for good follow-up. As we've already discussed, David, with our Vision Day we issue a report and have follow-up sessions built into the process.

Wright

So, what are the major mistakes people make when they create a blueprint for their lives?

Berkley

The first mistake is when someone doesn't take the time to consider his or her future. From there on, it is important to prepare thoroughly and sufficiently.

The next mistake is that people try to pack in too much in a day. They run out of energy before they can create a comprehensive plan that's grounded in reality.

Very often there is not a logical progression from where people are now to where they want to go. If people try to do a lot of this work by themselves without a coach or facilitator, we joke that it's like trying to pick yourself up by your own hair! Doing a strategic planning session alone just doesn't work as well as having someone guide you along the way.

There are other mistakes, too. People create goals that are just too small or uninspiring. Conversely, they also create goals that are too large—so large that the goals are daunting—which makes it very hard to accomplish or to even get started on them. People also make a mistake of not having a way to validate their thinking and their ideas. They operate in a vacuum.

Very often we see people who conduct or arrange their own strategic planning day, but don't do it in a location conducive to relaxing and thinking deeply. The locations they choose are not inspiring or comfortable, and they then allow themselves to be interrupted or disturbed. Cell phones are a no-no when you are in the middle of sorting out your life!

Lastly, people don't find ways to ensure solid follow-through for themselves. A good plan must include a way to track progress and then celebrate it.

Wright

I can see how it would be easy to get off track if someone doesn't keep those important things in mind. So what makes a process like Vision Day so effective?

Berkley

Time away—out of the "bubbling pot"—for starters! Vision Day participants arrive on Martha's Vineyard or in Naples to a peaceful, inspiring location where they can sit down, relax, and be free of distractions. Debbie or I guide them through a series of questions and exercises to uncover their deepest desires, what they really want to have or do with their life. The process is effective because participants develop a complete plan that takes them from where they are to where they want to be with steps included that are appropriate at a level of detail that they can easily move forward to achieve.

During Vision Day, participants don't even have to take notes. And this is essential for any experience like this. Participants should be able to sit back and talk and think—to close their eyes and put their feet up, and in that way be fully present and comfortable. They also have someone with them as needed to help them see their truth. And even though the mechanisms and processes behind Vision Day are sophisticated, from the standpoint of the participants, Vision Day feels like a very simple process. It's fun, too. We've found there's quite a bit of laughter during Vision Day!

Wright

I can imagine how nice it would be to just sit and relax and have someone guide me through a process like this, wow. So how did you develop this process?

Berkley

My partner, Debbie, originally created it while sitting in a corporate retreat. She realized she'd participated in and led numerous work-related vision retreats but never one about her own life. She wondered, "If companies can have vision retreats, why shouldn't people have one for themselves? Their lives are at least as important, if not more so, than a company's."

From that pivotal awareness she created a daylong strategic planning day originally called "A Day Away," which later became Vision Day, for clients in her own coaching practice. I soon joined her and further developed the curriculum we use today. Vision Day has evolved over the past nine years to include our own proprietary processes and tried-and-true approaches from the other disciplines in our backgrounds. Our goal is to be efficient, fun, and to ensure that people also have a great time crafting their plan!

My professional background before I was a full-time coach was entrepreneurial, leading organizations, running large operations and projects, and doing strategic planning. Debbie's experience included leadership positions in business and politics and government, as well as expertise in the media including radio, newspapers, and television.

David, when we started doing this work, the field of coaching was in its infancy. In order to create a program like this we had to blaze a trail and find new ways to do things. That is one of the things that makes Vision Day a completely unique experience. To create this program we had to incorporate knowledge and techniques from organizational development, systems thinking, executive education and adult learning and development, grief and healing work, and even Asian mediation and wellness approaches.

Wright

It's fascinating how you've managed to weave all of these ideas together to create something so unique and special.

Berkley

Thanks, David. Debbie and I actually use the Vision Day process for our own lives. Each year we look forward to giving each other a Vision Day—at a discounted rate, of course!

Wright

How would I or anyone else know whether we are ready for a strategic planning day?

Berkley

This is a frequently asked question, so we have developed a special, free report for people to learn whether Vision Day or a personal, strategic planning day would be helpful for them. They can e-mail me at specialreport@visionday.com and I will gladly send the report by e-mail or fax.

Wright

Great. Are there any other tips or thoughts that you'd like to give our readers today?

Berkley

I want to wrap up by noting that successful people invest heavily in themselves. Benjamin Franklin once said, "If a man empties his wallet into his mind, his wallet will never be empty." Successful people learn and grow and get support for themselves. They focus on their gifts, strengths, and talents and think carefully about where they want to focus their precious time and energy. And finally, an elder statesman of the personal development world, Jim Rohn, has a quote I also love: "Don't begin any day until it is complete on paper."

I believe that if your life is important to you, if you want to make the best life transition, if you want to make your dreams a reality or have a fantastic year, then take your lifetime management one step further. Don't begin any precious year of your life until it is complete on paper.

Wright

Well, this has been a fascinating conversation. Rob, I appreciate your taking this time today to answer all my questions. I have certainly learned a lot, and I am sure the readers of this chapter will also. Your discussion of Vision Day will give many of people a lot to think about.

Berkley

Thanks, David. I really appreciate your interest and the time you've spent discussing Vision Day here today.

About the Author

Rob Berkley is acclaimed for his ability to transform businesses and lives as an executive coach and business advisor. Throughout almost two decades he has coached Fortune 500 senior executives, business owners, start-up entrepreneurs, and professionals. He co-developed Vision Day®, a customized strategic planning session that helps people craft and fulfill inspiring personal and career visions. Rob's clients describe him as a blend of Yoda, Gandhi, and Perry Mason combining wisdom, clarity, kindness, and a touch of "The Force." He lives with partner, Debbie Phillips, on Martha's Vineyard and Naples, Florida, where they hold Vision Day workshops and retreats.

Rob Berkley
P.O. Box 786
West Tisbury, MA 02575
Phone: 508.696.4949
E-mail: Rob@visionday.com
www.visionday.com

Chapter 11

KEVIN LUST

THE INTERVIEW

David Wright (Wright)

We are visiting again today with Kevin Lust, an author and inspirational speaker who has dedicated his life to finding ways to make people's lives easier and more effective and to finding ways to share that information with as many people as possible. To that end, he has traveled literally around the world, speaking to groups in every state in the U.S. but one, as well as in *sixteen* other countries. Recently he has brought his life-changing tips and suggestions to a new role—serving as the Director of the Illinois Small Business Development Center at Lincoln Land Community College—in addition to maintaining his busy speaking schedule. We first visited with him a few years ago, in an interview published in *Mission Possible! Volume Two* and we are thrilled to speak with him again today.

Welcome Kevin!

Kevin Lust (Lust)

Hello, David. And I am thrilled to be with you again. Thank you for having me.

Wright

It is our pleasure, believe me. You know, I remember some of the great tips you've shared with us in the past and it seems to me that one of the most compelling points you've discussed is the necessity of living your life with integrity. How did you decide that was important?

Lust

It was less a decision than it was a discovery really.

Wright

Most worthwhile things are, aren't they?

Lust

That's for sure. For me, the discovery came after being bombarded with headline after headline about major corporations and the individuals in them living their lives without integrity. For months and now years, the only news we saw about business was about the scandalous—and I use that word literally—behavior of some of the top executives of the business world. From Enron to Tyco to Worldcom and even Martha Stewart, we were showered with descriptions of activity that these people would not have wanted shared in the polite company of a few of their closest friends, let alone plastered on the front page of the *Wall Street Journal.* Yet, these paragons of leadership, the "best" their companies could offer, chose to engage in maneuvers that couldn't pass a smell test in a hog barn, not to mention an independent audit.

Wright

It was amazing to me how widespread these scandals seemed to be. For a while there it felt like we were hearing about a new company that was affected nearly every week. Do you think what we were seeing is common in corporate America today?

Lust

Not at all. Unfortunately, doing the right thing isn't newsworthy, and I hope it never is, so we don't hear about the good companies. By far the great majority of businesses and businesspeople follow the rules and usually play fair. I'll admit that their motivation for doing so is often less about morality than it is about fear of being caught, but the results are still legal if nothing else. I am concerned that a willingness to cut corners is becoming more and more accepted in the way we do business and in the way we live our lives.

Wright

Have you seen examples of that?

Lust

Sadly, too many. An example of one that I thought was fun was a situation I ran into at one of my many hotel stays while on a speaking tour. Walking into my room in a chain hotel in Salinas, Kansas, I came across a small plastic placard in the bathroom. The text read in part, "Due to the popularity of our guest room amenities, our Housekeeping Department now offers these items for sale." It then went on to list prices for everything from the towels to the blow dryers to the blankets. It even listed prices for the pillows (although it seems unimaginable to me that someone would actually want to take a used pillow from a hotel room). The final sentence read, "Should you decide to take these articles from your room, we will assume you approve a corresponding charge to your account."

Now, it took me a second, but then I realized what this little card really was saying. This hotel was having so much trouble with people taking things from their rooms that they had to assume that everyone would consider stealing things and needed to be warned. I have to confess that I was shocked by that and then a little irritated, to be honest. I mean, weren't they saying that they suspected I might be a thief? That made me a little mad. In fact, I was so mad that I stole their little plastic card!

Wright

(Laughs) That showed them!

Lust

For sure. Well, what it showed me, in all seriousness, was an unfortunate window on the world. Items in a hotel room are someone's property, and yet our standards have fallen so much as a society that we have to remind people not to steal them. You walk into a room and things are there that don't belong to you. How sad it is that someone has to remind us to leave those things there when we walk out.

Wright

It becomes a matter of trust, doesn't it?

Lust

A matter of trust and much more, in my opinion. You see, the issue initially rests on the fact that the opportunity to take these things so obviously is present. In fact, one probably could "get away" with taking a few little unpaid-for souvenirs from most hotels. The real question, though, is what are you getting "away" with? If you're trying to get away without paying, you probably will. If you're trying to get away without prosecution, you might succeed. But if you're trying to get away without negative consequences, you never can.

The consequences are that you know you have done something wrong and that doesn't change whether anyone else knows it or not. The title of my most popular keynote address right now is "Integrity Means Doing Your Best When No One is Looking," and that is what people too often forget in today's world.

Wright

So the ability to get away with something doesn't determine whether you should do it or not.

Lust

Not at all. In fact, if that question enters into the decision-making process, its very inclusion should indicate that what you're considering isn't the right thing to do.

Wright

That sounds a little like common sense to me.

Lust

To me, too. Unfortunately, in my travels, the most common thing I have found about common sense is how uncommon it is. Actually, I'm starting to think that most people must have a lot of common sense because I seldom see anyone using any of theirs up around me. It seems like they're hoarding it for later or something.

We probably shouldn't joke about it because the reality is that you, a lot of other people, and I have been blessed to have people in our lives who have taught us right and wrong. Others haven't, or they have forgotten the good lessons they might have learned.

Wright

You bring up an interesting point. Do you believe that the way we are raised determines how we will react when faced with tough choices between right and wrong?

Lust

Well, I'm not a trained sociologist—and I didn't even stay in a Holiday Inn Express last night—but, again, our friend common sense would lead one to believe that background and education absolutely play a role in determining our moral values. Understand, though, that we are not talking about obvious sins here, in most cases. Go back to the corporate challenges we talked about earlier. In most of those cases, individuals engaged in behavior that most outside observers viewed as outrageous after it was revealed, yet the perpetrators considered the behavior justifiable at some level when they chose to do it. Or at the very least, they were able to create a justification for it after the fact.

Wright

In my own life, I sometimes have caught myself trying to make excuses for things I've done that I knew at the time weren't necessarily the right things to do. Is making excuses the problem?

Lust

They are *a* problem, but not *the* problem. Making excuses may be our way of justifying behavior we know to be wrong, but the behavior itself stands as the real question. In fact, I've used a question on many occasions that has made my choices much clearer. I call it the *News-Tribune* test and it works like this. When faced with a questionable choice, I just ask myself if I would like a picture of myself doing whatever it is I'm thinking about doing to show up on the front page of the newspaper my parents read. The answer to that question will sober you up in a hurry.

Wright

It sounds like you are talking about setting some high standards.

Lust

Yes, in fact "Reaching Higher Standards" is the title of another one of my presentations. But, you know, they are not impossibly high standards by any means. Take an example we use in our programs.

In visiting with a group I am addressing as part of their convention or conference or whatever, I might ask them an intentionally off-the-cuff kind of question. I'll casually say, "Since I'm not from here, about how fast can you legally drive over the speed limit in this area?" Inevitably, the audience will respond with "five miles" over the limit, or "nine," or "ten." In fact, some joker will nearly always say, "twenty with a radar detector!" Of course, when I repeat the question stressing the *legally*, they realize that the answer is zero.

Now, am I suggesting that people absolutely must drive exactly the speed limit every time they take the wheel? No. My attorney friend, Don Tracy, helped me understand the difference between substantial compliance and strict compliance. In some laws, there is an expectation of rigid adherence, while other laws are written with an expectation that there is a range of behavior that still meets the standard of the law. You just can't murder someone, period, but driving a few miles per hour one way or the other of the speed limit probably meets the standard of substantial compliance. So, I am not expecting people to drive at exactly the speed limit. What I am asking people to be aware of is what their actions say if they choose to go faster.

What if your children are riding in the back seat when you choose to speed? You've told them all their lives to obey the law. Then, every time you jump in the car you disobey the law. This time are you telling them, "Obey the law, unless you can break it without getting caught," or is it, "Obey the law, unless everyone else is disobeying it"? Or are you indicating, "Obey the law, and if you can't, at least get close"?

Wright

That goes back to what you said before about making excuses, doesn't it?

Lust

It does. Kids are a lot smarter than we give them credit for being and they understand the messages that our actions send a lot more clearly than they do the lessons our words try to teach.

Wright

Your actions really do define who you are. So would you say that we should look at peoples' actions to understand them?

Lust

Absolutely. One of my favorite Lust Lessons is, "It's not what you say, it's what you show." Let's take an example from the world of sports. Columnist Ed Sherman reported a remarkable story in the *Chicago Tribune* a few years ago about golfer Jeff Sluman. During the Buick Open, Sluman had shot sixty-nine in each of the first two rounds of the tournament to put himself into position to challenge for the title. But, on the first hole of the third round, he noticed that the golf ball he was using lacked the Pro V1 markings that Titleist prints on the side of that model of ball. Although this was a manufacturer's error, and an extraordinarily rare occurrence, the result of those missing few tiny letters was that Sluman's ball was "nonconforming" in the eyes of the PGA. He was using an illegal ball as far as the rules were concerned. As soon as he noticed, Sluman reported the error to PGA officials and soon they informed him that he had been disqualified from the tournament—unfortunately right after he had eagled the fourth hole.

Now, no one else could have seen the markings on the ball. They are less than one sixteenth of an inch high! Jeff Sluman could easily have pitched the ball to a fan after a hole and no one would have known a thing. But *he* would have, and that was the difference. Sluman said, "I couldn't have looked anybody in the eye after that if I had thrown the ball to a kid and walked off. That's just not me."

Wright

That's a great story. I'll bet that makes a lot of golfers rethink some of the scores they've turned in.

Lust

I'm guessing too many of them. I believe the real essence of the story is captured in Sluman's comment. "That's not me," he said, and that's the beauty of it. He had made this decision a long time before he needed to. He had decided that he was a golfer who followed the rules. Then, when the situation presented itself, he didn't have to agonize over his options or dwell on the possibilities. He just said to himself, "This isn't right. I have to turn it in." It was a dead issue for him—nothing to worry about.

That's the lesson for all of us right there. If you decide in advance that you are going to do the right thing, then no matter what presents itself, your choice is made for you. I have devoted my studies and research for the last seventeen years of my life to finding ways to make peoples' lives easier and this is one of the most freeing tips I have ever come across. Sluman already had made his choice and his life was so easy for the next few holes of that tournament that he shot two under par on one hole. From the moment he told an official, he knew he eventually was going to be disqualified. Yet, while you have to believe that he was plenty upset about that, what never disturbed him for a minute was whether he had done the right thing. Do you know what he said about that? "Never a doubt. That's what separates our game from other games."

Never a doubt. Can you see how much easier that makes your life? Look, even if you can't get behind the moral importance of doing your best when no one is looking, don't miss the benefit that comes to you by making every decision you ever have to make automatically easier. It's like the guy who decides that if the traffic light turns yellow he'll stop every time. He has just eliminated a major stressor in the lives of anyone who drives in traffic. You know the feelings of doubt and anxiety you have when the light turns yellow—"Should I go or stop? Stop or go? Go? Stop? Go? Oh boy, looks like I better go. Woops, shoulda' stopped." You know how it goes. With the decision pre-made, the other guy just slows down if things are looking close and stops when the light turns yellow. I'm not sure the few minutes you might save by beating the first light ever offsets the minutes the extra stress shaves off your lifespan in the long run.

Wright

Obviously, not everyone makes the kind of good decisions that golfer Sluman did, whether in advance or not. Do you know of examples of decisions that didn't have the same results?

Lust

A very public example occurred at nearly the same time as Sherman reported the Sluman story, because it was just then that a judge sentenced Martha Stewart to jail.

Wright

I remember that.

Lust

Sure, most people do. What many people don't remember, though, are the particulars of why she went to jail. Martha Stewart sold about 4,000 shares of stock in a company called ImClone Systems Inc. that her friend, Dr. Samuel Waksal, lead. Now, it seems that Waksal was selling his ImClone shares after getting a tip that federal regulators were not going to approve ImClone's anti-cancer drug, and Stewart's stockbroker was accused of ordering his assistant to tell Stewart that. If that happened, it is insider trading and that is against the law.

Martha was not convicted for insider trading, but she did make the trade and the court found that when investigators questioned her about it later, she made false statements to them. The court convicted Martha Stewart of two counts of that, along with conspiracy and obstruction of justice, and sentenced her to jail.

Here's what bothers me about all this. Martha Stewart formerly was a stockbroker! She had to know that the circumstances surrounding this whole deal didn't smell right, and I have to believe that a little bit of Jeff Sluman's attitude could have saved her a whole lot of grief, worry, and image rebuilding. If she had decided in advance that she would not make deals even remotely based on inside information, nobody would have ever heard of ImClone and we're all spared the "Martha redecorates her prison cell" jokes.

Wright

And there were plenty of those. So, what lessons should we learn from all this?

Lust

Well, the first lesson is to determine your values before you need them. If you know what is important to you and what lines you will not cross, you'll find that the words "ethical dilemma" seldom need to enter your vocabulary.

Just as importantly, though, is to remain ever vigilant for times when you might be skirting those values or letting your standards slip.

Wright

It's easy to take short cuts, right?

Lust

And those short cuts can lead to some really nasty—even tragic—results. NASA even coined a phrase for it. They call it "normalization of deviance." Not exactly about cutting corners, this refers to the acceptance of events that are not supposed to happen. When a horrific fireball destroyed the space shuttle Challenger in 1986, investigators traced the problem to leaking O-rings that allowed "blow-throughs" of hot gas to escape from joints in the ship's solid rocket booster. When Challenger was approved for launch on a morning with temperatures near freezing, the O-rings' rubber was more brittle and more susceptible to blow-through. But here's the thing: everybody knew that. They had had the problem in the past, however, and nothing particularly bad had happened, so they accepted it.

Years later, the shuttle Columbia was lost after foam insulation fell from an external fuel tank and caused damage to the craft's wing. Once again, here's the thing: foam had fallen off that tank on many previous flights, but someone decided to ignore the problem. No one designed these ships to have hot gas leaking out of sealed joints, and they certainly were not supposed to have pieces falling off them. But because flights had worked even though these problems had occurred, no one, or at least not the right people, addressed them. The problems were accepted. And there is your definition of normalization of deviance. Engineer Robert Kennedy called it "an incremental descent into bad judgment."

Wright

So do you think the same thing happens to people?

Lust

I do. In fact, I have a simple and embarrassing example of my own. When we moved into our beautiful new home a few years ago, one of the things we noticed not long after we moved in was that the toilet paper holder in the powder room was loose. If you pulled too hard on the toilet paper, the whole works could end up in your lap. Now, I know this is a rather indelicate example, but bear with me. Although this was a simple repair to make, I just never got around to it. Eventually, we accepted that the toilet paper roll in the guest bathroom came off if you pulled too hard. Our family and close friends knew about it and we even warned unwary new visitors when we noticed them heading that direction.

Eventually, my wife and I were going to be hosting a party with many people attending who would be making their first trip to our house. We knew we couldn't keep up with all of them, we really didn't want all these new visitors tearing up the toilet paper roll, and so I finally fixed it. It only took about twenty minutes, although it's loose again, by the way (I'm hardware-challenged).

So, there's a simple example of the acceptance of events that are not supposed to happen. I'll bet that if most people were honest, they could name two or three or more little problem areas at home that are not supposed to be the way they are, but that have come to be accepted. And those things are not a big deal. But, let me ask you something: what about the things that *are* a big deal? What about the bad habits you have let creep into your work routine that you know don't belong but that you let continue? What about the unresolved trouble spots that you have let sneak into your relationships that you know you should address before they get worse but that you continue to ignore? This is what happened to NASA. They said to themselves, "Boy, that foam ain't supposed to fall offa' there,"—and I paraphrase, I'm sure—but they kept flying and the foam kept falling. So, what kind of "foam" is falling around your life? What kind of home improvement have you been ignoring? What sort of bad habits are you letting get worse?

Wright

Wow, that is a lot to think about. People are probably checking their job jars even as we speak. What do you think causes people to accept the parts of their life that they know they shouldn't accept?

Lust

NASA researchers cited three main villains that we could probably apply to ourselves as well. First, they noted what they called a "production of culture," which they defined as the teaching and practice of methods that aren't effective. Then the researchers referred to a "culture of production," which pushed NASA workers to get the job done, no matter what. Finally, they identified "structural secrecy," which led to a world where things could be gotten away with.

Personally, I think most of us can find many of those circumstances in our own lives. Most of us encounter people who do cut corners and don't mind telling us how they did it. In fact, they may even make fun of the people who do try to do the right thing. We can find the production of the culture of short-changing ourselves and the rules virtually anywhere we care to look.

It also is easy to fall into a trap formed by the culture of production. When production at any cost becomes the goal, integrity easily can be set aside. I suspect this was one of the problems at Enron. Producing positive earnings numbers quarter after quarter to support an unsustainable stock price led top decision-makers inside one of the biggest corporations in the world to make some really bad decisions about how to achieve those earnings.

Structural secrecy leads people to think they can get by with things. You know, that happens every day, everywhere, more times than we might care to believe. It's why people speed, it's why people cheat on their taxes, and it's why people keep the money when they get too much change back at the store.

Wright

Kevin, I hate to say it, but you're almost depressing me *(laughs).*

Lust

Ah, but it all leads to the encouraging part. You see, it still is news when people do the wrong thing. And people still go to jail when they break the law. And even the richest and most powerful in our country can be brought to justice if they've earned it.

Bringing up some of these negative examples is just a way to help people see the importance of this discussion. When we say that integrity means doing your best when no one is looking, it really means, more than anything else, that you don't want to cheat yourself. It has less to do with cheating or doing something illegal than it has to do with shortchanging yourself—with doing less than your best.

Wright

So we want to use those examples to remind ourselves of how easy it is to slip and how important it is to do better.

Lust

That's right. One of my favorite quotes is from Ben Herbster, who said, "The greatest waste in the world is the difference between what we are and what we could become." That always reminds me of some of the questions business philosopher Jim Rohn asks: How tall does a tree grow? How long does a tortoise live? How far does a river flow?

The answers to those questions are as tall/long/far as it can. One could make the argument that humans are one of the few living organisms on earth that will settle for being something less than what we could be. "Good enough" is an insidious disease that afflicts humans but that seldom exists in nature. We accept less than our best more often than we should.

Wright

It sounds like you are asking a lot from people.

Lust

First, what I am asking is for people to ask a lot from themselves. Second, what I am asking people to ask of themselves is not *more* than they can do. It is *as much* as they can do. We don't want anyone to fall short of everything they can be or do. I believe the way to ensure this is to maintain high standards in those areas of your life that are important.

That part makes this attainable. I certainly am not asking anyone to be perfect, or even to try to be. My suggestion is this: in those areas of our lives that are important to us, we should set high standards of performance for ourselves. Then, on a day-to-day, minute-by-minute, second-by-second basis, we should work to meet and exceed those standards. And whether or not anybody else is checking up on us or even noticing us should not matter—we live up to those standards for ourselves alone.

Wright

And we could apply that in every area of our lives, couldn't we?

Lust

You bet. When I first was developing this program, I was working with salespeople. These lessons absolutely applied in that world because most of them were quite independent and operated with little direct supervision. So, if they weren't disciplined enough to do their best even without someone checking up on them, they wouldn't eat. They may have filled out their sales score sheets at the end of the month, but what they filled them out with was the work that they did from the first day forward.

Think about that in a family. You don't get to start being a good mother or father at some preordained point in your child's life. You can't say, "Okay, when the kid starts understanding me, that's when I'll start talking to him" or "when she's old enough to read, I'll start reading to her." And you had better not wait until they're old enough to drive to start teaching them how to be independent. To be a good parent, you have to do it all the time. And that's true about being a good spouse or child yourself or friend or coworker or uncle or aunt or godfather or . . . well, you get the picture.

Wright

How would you suggest someone get started on the path to setting and reaching high standards?

Lust

The first step is to determine in what areas you want or need to establish these standards. For example, as much as I might want to, I just haven't been able to assign a high priority to how our yard looks. I like our yard to look nice, I like working in the yard, and I feel embarrassed when things start looking shabby. But we just have too many other things going on to give the yard the attention that it deserves and we have been unwilling to give up the cash it would take to pay someone else to give our yard that much attention. I'd rather spend it on our family. So, if you drive past our house, you might see some grass that needs cutting, or some bushes that need trimming, or even something growing out of the gutter occasionally. That is where we have chosen to devote less of our energy. Alvin Toffler said, "The most important expression of excellence is excellence in choosing the actions in which to excel." So, we choose not to excel in lawn grooming.

For those areas in which you decide to excel, we want you then to define what excellence means—the goal-setting that wonderful experts like Brian Tracy tell us about—and then to develop a list of the behaviors that will be necessary to reach those goals. Then (and here's the tough part) you have to behave that way.

Wright

It sounds simple.

Lust

It is simple, but it is not easy. And that's why I think it is so important to stay vigilant about how we are performing relative to our standards. I don't believe that employees at places like Enron started off saying to themselves that they were going to defraud the company and its shareholders of billions of dollars. I think somebody probably discovered a gray area in an interpretation of a rule that allowed them to do something that might have been the least little bit questionable. Then, once they found themselves in that gray area, it got harder and harder to distinguish shades, and eventually they couldn't even see the ethical lines they were crossing. Once they crossed those lines though, it seems like they decided it would be better to hope nobody would notice than to go back and repair what they had done.

That's the slippery slope of cutting corners. Once you've shaved the edges on one corner it becomes easier to do it again and again after that. Pretty soon, shaved corners become the standard and the nice square ones look out of place. Four miles over the speed limit becomes the new speed limit and then it's, "Why don't we just go a few miles over that?" And on it goes.

Instead of starting down that slope, why not set standards for yourself that keep you from slipping? Live up to those standards and don't cheat yourself. That's when you start enjoying all the success you can.

Wright

Well, Kevin, you've given us a great deal to think about and some powerful lessons to pursue. We appreciate your visiting with us, and I look forward to visiting with you again.

Lust

Thank you. I always enjoy it.

Wright

We've been visiting with inspirational speaker and great thinker Kevin Lust, author of *Financial Fitness: How to Budget Your Time, Your Money, and Your Life*. We hope you've enjoyed our conversation as much as we have.

About the Author

A professional speaker and trainer since 1990, Kevin Lust has delivered nearly 1,800 presentations in sixteen countries on four continents. He is the Founder and President of Lust Development Group, Inc., an organization dedicated to helping people live their lives more effectively. Kevin is a Certified Speaking Professional, and serves as the Director of the Illinois Small Business Development Center at Lincoln Land Community College.

Kevin has authored two best-selling audio learning albums, "Coaching Skills for Mangers and Supervisors," and "Financial Fitness," along with chapters in three business anthologies. He enjoys life in Springfield, Illinois, with his wife and son.

Kevin Lust
Lust Development Group, Inc.
Phone: 888.241.5878
E-mail: kevinlust@kevinlust.com
www.kevinlust.com

Chapter 12

JAY WALLUS

THE INTERVIEW

David Wright (Wright)

Today we're talking with Jay Wallus. He began his selling career the hard way eighteen years ago when he was hired to head out to the streets of Boston to pick up business by door-to-door cold calling in the office equipment industry. He quickly rose to be one of the top sales reps in the country, not because of his great closing skills but because he thought "out of the box" and developed creative strategies to fill his sales funnel. A true entrepreneur at heart, Jay founded Street Smart, his sales and marketing consulting company, to show business owners and salespeople alike that the key to selling more is simply learning unique ways to get in front of more qualified prospects.

Jay, welcome to *Speaking of Success.*

Jay Wallus (Wallus)

Thank you David, it's nice to be here.

Wright

So you've worked with and met with hundreds of salespeople and entrepreneurs. What's the single most determining factor when it comes to people who succeed in business as well as in sales?

Wallus

One of the things I always found that successful salespeople and entrepreneurs did was that they actually acted on what they knew they "should" do. This is a whole new ballgame because everyone "knows" what to do or they've heard something or they've listened to a tape or read a book. The very successful people actually took what they learned *and acted upon it.* They didn't blame circumstances, they didn't blame the economy or the market—they always found a way to make things happen.

Wright

I find a lot of salespeople and business owners don't have much to say when I ask them why I should do business with them. In fact, almost every time I ask I hear something like, "Great service," or "We've been in business since 1973," which isn't all that compelling a statement to me. How do you help your clients with a problem like that?

Wallus

I work with them to develop a Unique Selling Proposition (USP).

An example of a good "unique selling proposition" is FedEx. Their unique selling proposition is: "When your package absolutely, positively has to get there overnight." The first FedEx salesperson who walked through a prospective customer's door and said, "Hi, my company delivers packages and letters," got the manager's response which was, "No thank you, we have the post office." It was then that the salesperson made the unique sales proposition and said, "What if I can guarantee it overnight?" That gives the customer a reason to buy.

Another wonderful example is Domino's Pizza: "Delivered in thirty minutes or less or it's free." That's absolutely a huge, unique selling proposition. There are places everywhere that sell pizzas but Domino's took that regular product and put a very unique spin on it that made it very appealing for people to buy. They created a huge franchise as a result.

Another great opportunity for a USP is (believe it or not) water. How did water get a USP? People filtered it, took out the impurities, and now sell it for $2.50 a bottle.

So instead of "We've been around twenty years," or "We have great people," or "We're customer driven," a unique selling proposition will make a business *go through the roof.* The key thing here is to remember *that time must be set aside* to build and develop the USP. If that isn't done, the product or service will fall into the commodity box—not good.

Wright

You're always emphasizing that salespeople should educate their clients and prospects. What exactly do you mean by that?

Wallus

When you educate people about your industry, you become the guru in your industry. If you write an article and it appears in a trade journal, you become a "guru" in your industry. If you're out speaking in front of clients for a certain industry or you do a presentation for Chamber of Commerce groups or Rotary Clubs, you become the guru. The most important thing when you're educating people is to understand that as you go through that process, *you are becoming the guru—the authority—in your industry.* In order to be unique and different, you don't just sell your product or service (like everyone else), you *must* teach them how to use or consume it in the most efficient manner possible. The people who educate their clients about their industry are the ones perceived as gurus plain and simple. Everyone else is only interested in the sale, but you're the one who's showing them how to use and best *benefit* from your product or service—there's a *big* difference.

Wright

I've heard that you have referred to people as lemmings—the rodents that because of their periodic population spurts and declines gained a mythological reputation for hurling themselves *en masse* off the edge of cliffs. What caused that connection?

Wallus

I learned about the lemming probably around ten years ago. It just amazed me that these creatures kill themselves by the hundreds of thousands. What happens is they gather in massive numbers and each follows the other to its death *without thinking.*

I think that people often act like lemmings instead of human beings who have the power, creativity, and the knowledge to be different. If someone else in their industry puts an ad in the Yellow Pages that says "three convenient locations," or "we have friendly customer service," or "we've been around since 1925," readers will follow that ad in the Yellow Pages or in their company's brochure. Even though the other people's ads, haven't worked historically, and still don't work now, *people will just follow other people in the industry because they think it's the right thing to do.* What I try to emphasize is let's not be a lemming, let's *not* follow the crowd, and let's find out what's working and use our brain and use all our imagination and knowledge to come up with much different strategies than the rest of the "herd."

Wright

Jay, it seems if I constantly hear salespeople and business owners say the best way to get business is through referrals. I know you cringe when you hear people say that. Why do you have that type of reaction?

Wallus

It's interesting because when I interview prospective clients and ask them what methods they currently use to bring in new customers, I often hear them say, "Well, I do a lot of business by referral." I will then ask, "Can you tell me more about that?" They tell me that every once in awhile someone mentions the name of that person's company to someone else and that person will call the company and will buy a product or service. The reason why I cringe is that it's a very knee-jerk reaction to the question. In reality, they "hope" these referrals come in by having their customers talk about them.

What I try to do with my clients is to implement a referral generating *system* that runs inside the business just like paying the bills, taking count of the inventory, and keeping track of accounts receivable. It actually becomes part of the business itself.

Wright

I know that you talk about leverage. Will you tell our readers about some of the ways you've helped salespeople and business owners use technology to create leverage?

Wallus

Sure, I'd be happy to. Most people have some sort of a customer relationship management program (CRM). It could be either ACT! or Goldmine, or even Outlook. Right now, that's probably extremely low-hanging fruit. What I like to work with clients now on, in order to leverage their time as much as they can to pick up new clients, is educating them about how to work with *auto-responder systems*. Auto-responder systems come into play when a client inquires about your product or service. What we do is set up an *entire sequence* of e-mails, letters, and faxes that are triggered automatically by that initial inquiry. What I mean by that is, now we're going to take our educational aspect (to become the guru) that I spoke about earlier, and we're going to send the clients an *educational* e-mail, letter, or fax periodically on an on-going basis. These aren't meant to be sales pitches, they are ways to *educate* them to use the product or service easier, *even if they haven't purchased it yet.* When we do this, we're becoming more of a guru. I've found time and time again that when you approach prospects in this manner, you're much more likely to get more clients down the road.

The number one mistake most business owners make is they simply don't follow through for for a long enough period of time They stay in touch for a little while and then the prospect falls through the cracks. That's what today's technology can do and it will absolutely, positively solve that problem.

Wright

That coincides with what I've heard about failure. I've read many times and many people say that 98 percent of failure is caused by quitting. And not following up would be quitting, wouldn't it?

Wallus

Yes, absolutely. But if you had a system in place it would follow up for you.

Wright

When you see salespeople and business owners take the ideas and strategies you have mentioned here and put them to use, what typically happens?

Wallus

It's almost as if the business owner looks at me and says, "I can't believe it could be this easy." The one thing they needed to do is take action on it. It's almost as if they get a new feeling for the business and the industry because as the owner, they get excited when the business grows and they add new clients. When I see that change happen in them mentally, they seem to enjoy the business much more. As long as they see clients coming in, they're happy. Then generally we'll go to work on refining the process. It's almost like a mental awakening for them—they find that passion again for their industry. That passion, energy, and love for their business had disappeared when they got bogged down and started to focus too much working in the business rather than on it and bringing new clients in.

Wright

In the beginning I mentioned you got your start selling door-to-door, cold calling in the office equipment industry. Along the way, who did the most to influence you and help you? Did you have any mentors—anyone who made you who you are today?

Wallus

I've never met the gentleman, but Napoleon Hill, author of *Think and Grow Rich,* is the first person who comes to mind. I have the original book that I bought. It's tattered and many pages are marked in it. That was almost my go-to manual when I was experiencing a challenge or having a tough day. It really taught me how to *think differently,* which is what I work with salespeople on. I tell them to try to think differently about a certain situation.

Wright

Well, what a great conversation. I really appreciate all the time you've taken with me today to answer these questions. I think these answers will help our readers understand more about how to become successful.

We've been talking with Jay Wallus. Listening to him today, I think he has some new ways to look at things and some different techniques to help people drastically grow their business.

Jay, thank you so much for being with us today on *Speaking of Success.*

About the Author

Jay Wallus began his selling career the hard way eighteen years ago when he was hired to head out to the streets of Boston and dig up business by door-to-door cold calling in the office equipment industry. He quickly rose to be one of the top sales reps in the country—not because of his great closing skills but because he thought "out of the box" and developed creative strategies to fill his sales funnel.

A true entrepreneur at heart, Jay founded Street Smart, his sales and marketing consulting company, to show business owners and salespeople alike that the key to selling more is simply learning unique ways to get in front of more qualified prospects.

Jay's own compelling journey of persistence through fear and uncertainty as he went through all of the usual setbacks that salespeople and entrepreneurs face allows him to share his own unique experiences with others. No other speaker blends this powerful mix of commonsense strategies, creative thinking, and high energy to help salespeople and entrepreneurs understand what it takes to overcome the everyday hurdles that stop most people dead in their tracks.

Jay Wallus
Street Smart
Baldwin Park I
12 Alfred Street, Suite 300
Woburn, MA 01801
Phone: 781.245.6800
Fax: 781.245.6810
E-mail: jwallus@streetsmartbizdev.com
www.streetsmartbizdev.com

Chapter 13

CHARLES PARRISH

THE INTERVIEW

David Wright (Wright)

Today we're talking with Dr. Charles Parrish. Dr. Parrish has spent most of his thirty-year career in the non-profit sector and was a CEO/Executive Director over half of that time. His most recent venture has been as a speaker and consultant to business, education, and government leaders and currently he is the President of the Foundation for Futures in Medicine, a nonprofit organization dedicated to bringing more multicultural students into the field of medicine. His particular interest today is the question of innovation. He sees the ability to be innovative as crucial to a given company or organization's success as well as the key to keeping American businesses and the American economy the world's strongest.

Dr. Parrish resides in Atlanta with his wife of twenty-four years and their two children.

Dr. Parrish, welcome to *Speaking of Success.*

Dr. Charles Parrish (Parrish)

Thank you very much.

Wright

Why do you think that innovation is so important today?

Parrish

Well, David, number one, I think it's the simple realization that the world has changed. Today Toyota, not General Motors, is really the number one automaker in the world. Toyota's stock keeps going up and General Motors' stock keeps going down, and I think today Toyota might even produce more cars. The world has changed. Technology has given us instant everything. It makes the pace so fast that it is hard to keep up.

I think the issue of innovation then comes down to whether or not a company is willing to be a good company or a great company. Good companies tend to copy others. Great companies tend to innovate. Innovative companies tend to be the ones that everybody wants to emulate.

There is an organization called the Council on Competitiveness that is dedicated to seeing America succeed through innovation. Allow me to share a quote from them, "Investment in knowledge creation and innovation is critical to prosperity in an advanced economy and boosts the productivity growth that underpins a continually rising standard of living." I think they are absolutely right. This is an organization whose Board is made up of people like the presidents of Georgia Tech and the University of North Carolina, and the CEO of IBM. Those are the kinds of people who make up the Board of the Council on Competitiveness because they understand that investment in knowledge creation and innovation are the keys to success in the twenty-first century.

It's coming up with new ways to look at things and then understanding that there are new ways and better ways to be able to do things that gives the great companies an edge. That is what currently gives the American economy an edge. But when you think about the fact that the number of engineering grads in the United States is a declining number (and has been a declining number for well over ten years) and that China is producing nine times the number of engineers that we are (and we'll never match their sheer numbers), then making the most of our "Yankee ingenuity"—our cultural heritage of innovation—will be crucial in maintaining ours as the greatest economy in the world.

Innovation is the key factor in keeping the American economy number one in the world and giving us an increasingly stronger standard of living. But the sad part is if you put twelve random CEOs from any American companies in a room and you ask them when was the last time their company, or even an individual within their company, developed a new product or technology, almost without exception they say never—it's never happened. And that concerns me. So I think that helping business leaders and organizational leaders understand how crucial it is for them to really embrace innovation as a means of doing what they do is extremely important.

Wright

But how does innovation relate to non-profits, education, and other non-manufacturing businesses and organizations?

Parrish

Well, that's a good question. The question comes because most people have the wrong idea when they think about the word "innovation." Typically, when you say or think about the word "innovation," people think of gadgets—the hottest new thing at the computer store—or they think of iPods or BlackBerry phone accessories. Those are all products of innovation, but gadgets are only one part.

The current CEO of IBM is a fellow named Samuel J. Palmisano. He said something remarkably intuitive. He said, "The way you will thrive in this environment is by innovating—innovating in technology, innovating in strategies, and innovating in business models." Here is a guy who is the CEO of the ultimate high tech company, IBM, and two of the three things he said had nothing to do with technology but with strategies, business models, methodology—how you do what you do.

Non-profits, education systems, and government agencies too often fall into a rut of how they go about doing the task of reaching their goal. They become seemingly incapable of change. So when their non-profit fundraising or their organizational structures or their growth strategies (if they even have one) become frozen, then they realize they are stuck. But they want to maintain the way they've been doing things and that this how things have to be done. Suggest a new approach and often the response is, "We ain't never done it that way before." So as a result, nonprofits are not reaching their goals, they are not maximizing their potential, and they are not raising the kind of funds they could be raising.

In the same way, government agencies are often not reaching and serving the people in the best way that they could. If it's an education system, they are not producing the kind of graduates they need to be producing, simply because they find it so difficult to change their strategy or to change their business model. Too many of the these organizations are doing things essentially the same way they did thirty, forty, or fifty years ago and they are wondering why their memberships are declining, why their financial contributions are flat at best, and why their end-product is inadequate.

If non-profits, education systems, and government agencies could understand that innovation is not just technology but also developing new and innovative strategies, business plans, and methodologies then they would begin to discover just how effective they could be.

Wright

So if innovation is so obviously important, aren't most companies and organizations today putting it into practice?

Parrish

Well, no they are not. They are paying a lot of lip service to it. They are very interested in it. But no, most companies are really not putting innovation into practice and there are a lot of different reasons as to why. Whether it is a for-profit company or a non-profit organization, those reasons tend to be pretty much the same.

Very often they are just change resistant—they feel very threatened by the uncertainty of what change is going to bring. They ask questions such as, "How we are going to do something new?" "I don't know—I'm not sure I'm happy with that." "Who knows if it is going to work or not?"

Often cost is a factor. That is *the* number one reason American carmakers give as to why they are in trouble. They've known for years the changes they need to make, but they've been unwilling to pay the cost to either renovate their assembly line systems or build new factories, so they just continue to largely do what they've always done.

A lot of it is just arrogance—just pure arrogance. "I know what I know. I make money every year. I am successful at what I do. There's nothing out there I need to know." So they just don't want to hear and they don't even want to consider possibly doing things in an innovative way that would be better than what they are currently doing because they're not teachable.

That leads to the last point I want to make on this. This is the sad part—too often people are just comfortable with mediocrity. They are comfortable with sort of strolling along. They are comfortable with fair-to-good and yet they could be great. They could be great if only they would be willing to step out and try something different.

Wright

So how does a company or an organization become innovative?

Parrish

As with most things, it starts with leadership—it starts at the top. For companies that are innovative, their leaders are very different than companies that are not. Number one, the leaders of innovative companies recognize that they cannot micromanage the company. You have to be willing to give the people below freedom to work, freedom to try new things, freedom to work outside the box, and even the freedom to fail. And so the leaders of innovative companies understand that they cannot micromanage what their company does.

Number two is if somebody is going to be an innovative leader then the question is, in what direction is he or she going to lead? Leaders of innovative companies recognize that the way they need to go is to develop a culture of innovation within their company. Within a culture of innovation is where new and innovative products, technologies, strategies, business plans, and methodologies just flow out of the course of a regular day's work. It just flows—it just happens—because employees are free to imagine and free to try to take what they imagine and make it real. The company's unspoken motto is "Dream, Make it Real, and Dream Again." That way you can constantly have a cycle of innovation going on within the life of a given company.

Tom Peters has a wonderful book titled *The Circle of Innovation.* It's a great title. It's a great book. It gets at the heart of what it means to lead a company like this and to see that a culture of innovation just naturally begins to percolate and produce new kinds of products, new strategies, and new technologies. And how that happens is they have the right leadership in place, the right employees in place, and the employees have the freedom to be able to make it work. But there is just one basic human element that is the key that most companies miss—it is simply listening.

Number three, the companies that have leaders who really do understand what it means to be an innovative company, understand the value of listening. Peters offers Proctor & Gamble, for instance, as a prime example of a great innovative company where leaders understand the value of listening. Way back, almost thirty years ago, they were one of the first companies to put a toll-free telephone number on all of their products. "Give us your feedback," they said. Today that toll-free number is one of *the* key sources of product development for Proctor & Gamble.

Listen to the people who use your product. Very often, for a lot of companies, their product users know more about their product than they do. If you make a copier, chances are the secretaries and the office workers out there who use the copier know more about it than you do. They know what kind of paper works best in it. They know what kind of toner works best in it. They know how to fix it if it breaks. They know your product inside and out. Listen to them.

Peters tells of one upper level leader of a high tech company in California who tells everybody he's off on vacation. (Well it's not a vacation really.) He takes two months out of the year, usually July and August, just to go and visit every single one of the company's clients. He also goes and visits a lot of the people his company would like to have as clients. He goes to the clients to listen to them as to how they use the company's products. In what ways are they using the products? What is it that the product does well? What is it that the product doesn't do well? Where does the product fail? Where does the product come up short? Where does their product excel?

He comes back with two months' worth of material and at that point he gives his report back to his company and turns his people loose with it. How do we make our product better? So listening is simply a huge, huge part of being innovative; but most companies don't listen well to the people who use their products.

Another great company in terms of being able to be innovative is 3M. This company has made a little bit of money from something called masking tape. They've sold a few cases of masking tape over the years. Masking tape was developed by a salesman who was calling on clients who were frustrated that there wasn't a product out there that would do what they needed to have done and so he went back and came up with the product just purely to make a couple of customers happy. Since then the company has been able to sell a few million cases of masking tape through the years.

So the three real keys then are:

1. Leadership
2. A goal of creating a culture of innovation

3. Listening—listening to your users, listening to your competitors; finding out from them what they are doing, what they are not doing, what makes them happy, what's got them frustrated, and then listening to what's happening out there in the world of technology. How can a technology that maybe is not even out there yet impact your business? How can you make better use of available technological resources?

If your company wants to be innovative, it should follow those basic three steps.

Wright

Will you give our readers an example of a company with a culture of innovation?

Parrish

Let me come back to 3M. The 3M organization is really my favorite "poster child" of what a company with a culture of innovation is really all about. A lot of people don't know what 3M stands for. It stands for the "Minnesota Mining and Manufacturing Company." Okay, Minnesota, got that. Manufacturing, yeah, but Mining? The company started out doing mining but very quickly they found they didn't have a buyer for what they were mining, so they started taking what they were mining and using it in their own manufacturing.

From the very beginning they had to be innovative because what they started out to be was primarily a mining company and then they had to shift and become a manufacturing company. The first product 3M ever produced was sandpaper from the materials they were mining. Then they went just in every direction possible because from the earliest stages of that company there was a culture of innovation—from reflective signs or road materials to every kind of tape you can imagine, to CDs and DVDs, copiers, Scotch Guard, and Astroturf (the artificial turf that athletes play on that is on football fields, baseball fields, and so forth).

You probably have a winter coat hanging in your closet made from "thinsulate"—another 3M product—the great ultra-thin, ultra-light, waterproof material that keeps you warm and dry. The 3M company has sold a few "Post-it" notes over the last few years. They make medicinal products and everything from topical creams to surgical supplies. They make parts for flat screen televisions. This is an amazing, amazing company.

They average 100 new products a year. Now how do they do that? They do it within a culture of innovation. The leaders of 3M built into their manufacturing and into their research and development a plan where literally 15 percent of an employee's company time is to be devoted to side projects. So if you are working for 3M in research and development, 15 percent of your time needs to be devoted to projects you are just developing on your own. It's pretty remarkable that a company's top leadership would encourage people to take 15 percent of their workweek and use it on doing something other than what the company hired them to do!

Secondly, they encourage something called pirating. If you're working in one department and another department has something you need—some resources you are missing—and if you can get away with it, you can go get it. Whatever it takes to be able to continue your project and to be able to make your little secret lab flow well, even if it means stealing from another department, then that's what you can do.

Third, somewhere along the line (and I wish I knew who at 3M first came up with this) they have a standing rule that no project can ever be killed or put in the trashcan. For example, let's say you're working on a side project and it looks like it may work and you pitch it to the powers that be but get no funding to take it to the main level, 3M never will ever totally kill it. They may put it on a shelf but they will never throw it out. They'll just leave it sitting there until someone comes along to pick it back up again. That's how "Post-it Notes" were invented.

Somebody came up with a glue that just did not glue well, it just wasn't tacky enough. At 3M they have different measures of tackiness and this glue just wasn't tacky enough so it sat on the shelf. They didn't kill the project, they didn't punish the guy who wasted money developing this glue that didn't stick well, they just put it on the shelf. Years went by and one day another researcher came up with a way to use it. He had been singing in his church choir and was frustrated that all the little pieces of paper he put in his church hymnal to mark the pages just kept falling out. He finally remembered the guy down the hall who had a glue that wouldn't stick well. He took a pad of paper, put glue on it, took it to church, and it not only kept the little pieces of paper in the hymnal, but it didn't tear the paper pages in the hymnal. Low and behold, everybody else in the choir wanted some of the sticky little pieces of paper. He went back to the office, made more pads and began spreading the pads around the office. Knowing he was on to something he pitched the pads to the company's leadership and that's where Post-it Notes came from! The 3M company came out all right on that deal. Here was a project that someone spent a lot of time and energy on, but wound up with a glue that didn't work. It just sat on the shelf.

Part of the genius of 3M is that the researcher wasn't punished for making a glue that wouldn't stick, he was actually in the long-term rewarded! Because 3M never kills a project, this glue that didn't stick well just sat on the shelf until somebody sometime later could come along with a better idea of how to put it to use.

The leaders of 3M have absolutely no idea what their new products are going to be in five years because today there is someone quietly working in a lab on a side project that may be the biggest product in 3M's history five years from now. That's just how they operate. The leaders of 3M are all very comfortable working that way. Who wouldn't want to work for a company like that? So they are able to get the best and brightest people to work for 3M. They really are a great model for any company considering taking steps toward creating a culture of innovation.

Wright

So what would hold a company or organization back from being more innovative?

Parrish

I think again it starts with the leadership—it starts at the top. To be willing to be innovative like that you've got to be a risk-taker. You've got to be willing to put money into projects that may or may not pan out.

Going back to 3M's glue that didn't stick well, they spent a lot of money on that and it looked like wasted funds for a long time. When they first began to pitch the idea of something called a CD to the powers that be, a compact disc just didn't look like anything they had ever produced before or seen before, but they were willing to take a risk.

Most people who are in leadership positions in corporate America today are not great risk-takers. They play it very, very safe—always "coloring within the lines"—and as a result they get a good return but not what they could be getting. They are not maximizing their potential. A lot of it has to do with cost. Companies are hesitant to step out and say it's not just a matter of working and thinking outside the box or recognizing that there is no box. They are hesitant to do things totally different than it has ever done before, and spend a lot of money to be able to totally redo how it does what it does. Companies' investors are not sure they want to spend that kind of money when there is no guarantee on the return. I understand all that, but please tell me, what in life is guaranteed? There is no such thing as an absolute guarantee on any investment that is made. What *is* guaranteed is that if you *don't* learn how to innovate, if you don't learn to see the value of knowing that whatever success you have today is going to slowly erode over time as other companies that are more innovative, more willing to take more risks than yours are passing you by and getting a larger market share, then slowly your company will become irrelevant and obsolete.

Companies have to be willing step out and take the chance. Their leaders have to be willing to stick their neck out and absorb some of the risks and they have to be willing to pay the costs to be able to keep up.

Wright

So if I'm a new CEO of a company or organization and I want to start being innovative, where do I begin?

Parrish

Well, I think number one you have to start with the person in the mirror—with the man or woman you see every day in your mirror. Begin by asking yourself, "Am I willing take to take my hands off some of the reigns, to be willing to free up my employees, and am I willing to take those kinds of risks? Am I willing to stick my neck out?" If you can answer, "Yes!" to all those questions, then where are you going to go? If you are going to be a leader, it all depends on the direction you are going to lead the company.

I think a CEO would be wise to go to school and learn from some of the companies that are very, very successful at innovative leadership. It would be very smart to look at companies like 3M, Proctor & Gamble, Johnson & Johnson, and Apple. Apple is currently the company that comes to everybody's mind when thinking of innovation. Who knew five years ago that everybody needed an iPod? Apple did and they were willing to take a chance that this would be an innovative piece of technology that had frankly more uses than even what they had originally envisioned. How people and companies are using iPods is encompassing a larger scope than what Apple had originally envisioned and that works fine for them.

So if you are going to be a new CEO of a company or organization and you want to get the company moving in the right direction, it is important to first understand that you don't have to reinvent the wheel. There are plenty of great examples out there. Go to school on how these companies do what they do. How does Wal-Mart do what it does in the retail area? How does BMW do what it does in the automobile area? How does Sony do what it does in the television, stereo, hi-tech area? Wouldn't we all like to be able to sell coffee like Starbucks? How do these companies do what they do? Everybody is down on the airlines these days, yet Southwest Airlines continues to do very, very well by being the most innovative airline out there. How do they do what they do?

The first thing then is to take a look at that person in the mirror. Are you really ready to step out and do this?

Secondly, again, understand that you don't have to reinvent the wheel. So often we think that creativity, imagination, and innovation comes from the outer edges. Back in the 1980s when all the dot com companies were popping up everywhere, everyone thought these companies were just so creative and innovative. When you think about the companies that I am talking about, companies like 3M, Johnson & Johnson, Proctor & Gamble and so forth, these are companies that are a hundred years old and yet they are still the leading companies in America when it comes to innovation, and they are the leading companies in the world in their fields. These are the companies to focus on. So "go to school" and study them, because most of the dot coms of the 1980s are out of business.

And thirdly, be willing to accept temporary setbacks and failures. Just because things may not go well right out of the gate and you may stumble coming off the starting block, this doesn't mean that it's a bad idea. It will be difficult in the beginning but once you get into it, once your employees begin to catch the vision, once your stockholders begin to catch the vision, once your constituents see what is happening, and once your client base, your customers, and your product users begin to see what you're doing and the direction in which you're going, it's going to work and it's going to work really, really well. Just take the long view that if you continue to follow this pattern and go down this path, it's going to pay off in the end. Remember, 3M failed as a mining company!

Wright

So once you become more innovative, how do you keep it going?

Parrish

I think that goes back to a lot of what Tom Peters has been saying going back twenty to twenty-five years when he wrote *In Search of Excellence* and now in his last two books, *Re-imagine* and *The Circle of Innovation.* It really is a cycle—a cycle you are constantly going round and round with. Simply because you are 3M and you have come up with Masking tape and clear cellophane Scotch tape, you could be successful. I suppose you can make a lot of money just purely doing nothing more than making clear cellophane Scotch tape, *but* if you're going to put a premium on innovation and growth, if you're not willing to settle for second best, if you're not happy with mediocrity, if you are not happy with just being good but you want to be number one—you want to be *great*—then you realize that you cannot just sit back and say, "Hey, twenty-five, thirty, forty, fifty years ago we developed Scotch tape." Dream! Make it real! Dream again!

You will constantly be in a cycle of innovation. You are constantly going, happy that the last thing went well but you will be constantly looking at what the next thing might be. You will be building on the successes of the past but constantly looking for those new opportunities out there. Again, you do that by listening. You constantly listen to your customers—your users. You listen to what they are saying, to what they are looking for, and what they need.

There is one other element. One person whose name I don't think I've ever heard referred to in respect to business and whom Americans in particular could learn a lot from is C. S. Lewis. C. S. Lewis, the Oxford don, the Christian writer who wrote so many remarkable, creative Christian books (*The Chronicles of Narnia, Mere Christianity, Till We Have Faces,* and many more) also wrote a whole series of science fiction novels. Lewis understood the value of creativity in just living out life day-to-day. If you're going to become more innovative and keep it going (and he certainly kept it going in his writing for fifty years), then creativity and innovation must become part of your lifestyle. People like Lewis, Edison, Thomas Jefferson, and the author of *Doonesbury,* Gary Trudeau, all discovered the value of training one's mind to be creative and innovative in day-to-day living.

This is done by constantly looking at the world around you and recognizing that reality is a poor way to look at the world. Use your imagination!

When I was growing up in the '60s and '70s, probably my favorite show on television was *Star Trek.* If you look at what Gene Roddenberry wrote about in the *Star Trek* television series, you will find that we have most of those things now. My cell phone will do more than Captain Kirk's communicator! So recognize that reality is simply a poor way to look at the world. Use your imagination; use your creativity as you look at the world around you.

There was that great line from Bobby Kennedy after the death of his brother. Bobby, quoting a poet, said, "Some people look at the world and ask why? Others look at the world and ask why not?" Okay, why not? Why not go to the moon? Why not have laptop computers? Why not have these things? If you can begin to dream it as a leader then you can begin to see it happen within your organization. Once you become a leader committed to innovation, you can keep it going by simply keeping the cycle going of listening and dreaming and of continually creating that environment of creativity—the environment of innovation within your company.

Wright

This is going to radically change how companies and organizations look in the future, isn't it?

Parrish

Yes and no. I think it will in one sense. I think structurally 3M and Johnson & Johnson are set up like most other companies, so structurally there may not be much change. But this approach is going to radically change how things work inside the day-to-day operations within a company. It's going to change the value that leaders put in certain positions. It's going to change the way that companies value their employees, even that employee working on the line and that employee making minimum wage. It's going to change how we value conversations within companies and how we value team-building within companies.

I know a wonderful lady who worked for a major American hi-tech company. What she did for the company was to go around doing team-building at their various production facilities. She finally got frustrated and quit because she would go in and spend a great deal of money, time, and energy building teams to make production more cost effective and efficient, but then the company would go in behind her and destroy the team and lay off everybody and totally want to reshuffle the deck so that the team she had just put together only had a shelf life of about two months. That's just a huge, huge mistake on the part of that company.

The reason leaders are continuing to chase Sony and others is that they keep shooting themselves in the foot because of the low value they place on their employees. So yes, putting innovation in practice is going to change how these companies function within their infrastructures dramatically. They cannot keep micromanaging. They are going to have to have leaders who are willing to let their employees do what they do best to let their team-building continue to grow and to function.

On the surface from a distance you're not going to be able to see a lot of difference. You're still going to have CEOs; you're still going to have departments and so forth. What happens within that and the flow back and forth horizontally between those departments and vertically between the hourly worker and the CEO is going to change and I think that is going to be a very, very positive change for American business.

Wright

What a great conversation, Dr. Parrish. I really appreciate your spending all this time with me answering these questions. You have certainly enlightened me and I'm sure you've done the same for our readers.

Parrish

You're very gracious, David, thank you very much. I look forward to doing it again.

Wright

Today we have been talking with Dr. Charles Parrish. He's a speaker and consultant to businesses, education, and government leaders and President of the Foundation for Futures in Medicine. His particular focus today has been the question of innovation and if you have read carefully, I think you're going to have to agree with him—I think he knows what he's talking about.

Thank you very much, Dr. Parrish, for being with us today on *Speaking of Success.*

About the Author

DR. CHARLES PARRISH is President of the Foundation for Futures in Medicine and has more than twenty-eight years of experience working with both large and small work environments and with volunteer and paid staff. Dr. Parrish's background includes an undergraduate degree from the University of Florida, a graduate degree from Southeastern Baptist Theological Seminary, and a doctorate from Southern Baptist Theological Seminary. He is a member of the prestigious National Speakers Association. Dr. Parrish's work in the field of reconciliation and conflict resolution, both nationally and internationally, has given him a broad perspective seldom found in contemporary life.

Dr. Charles A. Parrish
1495 La Fayette Court
Loganville, GA 30052
Phone: 770.554.4614
E-mail: navigatorconsult@aol.com

Chapter 14

JEAN FEDORA

THE INTERVIEW

David Wright (Wright)

Today we're talking with Jean Fedora. Jean is the founder of Edge to Success Enterprises, LLC, a company dedicated to delivering motivational and entertaining presentations to high school and college students. Jean is an award-winning speaker whose talent for connecting with young audiences has made her a much sought-after speaker at schools throughout the country. Her dynamic yet "real" approach has been instrumental in helping thousands of young people create plans of action to achieve success in life. Her company, Edge to Success Enterprises, LLC, partners with corporations in order to bring her powerful messages and proven success steps to schools free of charge.

Jean, welcome to *Speaking of Success.*

Jean Fedora (Fedora)

It's great to be here, David.

Wright

So, how would you define success?

Fedora

I believe that success is truly the result of taking action toward a goal. It's the active step. Contrary to popular belief, I don't believe that success is the achievement of a goal, but rather the personal commitment to achieve that goal. Success is the pursuit of happiness.

Wright

So it's the journey and not the destination?

Fedora

Absolutely and I believe, therefore, that successful people are people who don't back down. Successful people don't give up; they are people who are true to their talents and their gifts. They are true to their passions. They are people who can ultimately say that they have happiness in their day-to-day life. They go after the dream they deserve, they create opportunities for themselves, and they use their available resources.

Wright

I've heard it repeatedly down through the years that 98 percent of all failure is because of quitting.

Fedora

I agree with that. It certainly is tempting to cut our success short when the journey is long and tough. But each of us has had some sort of obstacle in life where we found a way to get around it, above it, or through it. I believe it's important to keep those personal accomplishments at the forefront of our minds. When faced with that temptation to quit, we can use those past experiences to push ourselves to continue forward. The most successful people are those who have refused to quit time and time again.

Wright

So do you think that the journey to be successful is different for students than it is for adults?

Fedora

The journey to success is similar for students and adults in the way that the temptation to quit when the going gets tough does not discriminate between young and old. What is different is that young people are at the beginning of designing their lives versus adults, so if they map it out—actually take some early success steps toward fulfilling their passion and purpose—they can put themselves in an extremely powerful position. That's why I like working with young people—I can help them to give themselves that edge.

Wright

I have a seventeen-year-old who will be a high school senior next year and then she'll be going off to college. What should she or any high school and college student be doing to be successful in his or her chosen career and life?

Fedora

First of all, good luck with your seventeen-year-old—that's a very exciting year!

Your daughter, and every high school student in America, needs to take some proactive rather than reactive steps towards her life goals. She can jump-start her success for college as well as for the rest of her life. These types of steps are "homework" and they're options. Designing your life can be the ultimate homework.

Wright

Tell me more about that.

Fedora

These action steps—life homework—are options for students. I think that pursuing success is examining options. It requires work. Not everyone is willing to do the work.

You mentioned yourself that 98 percent of the people are not willing to do the work. In my opinion, success is really a habit that can be formed. If that habit is established early, it can carry over for a young person to their grades at school, to college choices, and ultimately to their professional success.

Wright

In your presentations you speak of the "four action steps." Will you share with our readers what they are and how they impact success?

Fedora

The four action steps are for either a high school student or a college student.

The first step for students is to get involved in a club or a school activity that relates to an interest that they have. Joining a club or activity will build their skills to work with others and develop leadership skills.

The second step that is essential for a student is to get involved in community service. Community service gives students that edge of perspective toward seeing the bigger picture—the outside world—and how they can impact the outside world. It will give them a stronger perception of what their accomplishments can lead to as far as enhancing an entire community.

The third step that is important is to begin career networking. I suggest students find out about different events and functions that might relate to their career interest. For example, if a student is interested in becoming a nurse and there is an event happening in the community at a hospital for nurses, the student should show up. It's a bold step. The reality is that most young people do not take it upon themselves to find out about these kinds of events and attend them. What is the first impression that young person is making? He or she is showing motivation, determination, and focus. It's an opportunity for students to ask questions about the realities of a career in that field.

Career networking can lead to the last action step that is absolutely essential—doing an internship. No matter how old a student is there are always internship opportunities out there. There is a misconception that you have to be in college to start interning. Yes, there are some companies that may require an intern to be of a certain age, but there are so many leaders in companies who would love to have a very motivated young person helping out in the office or in their organization in some way.

That "in-person research" yields understanding of the work required in a given field and builds commitment to achieve the end result. If students intern, network, involve themselves in the community, and get involved in clubs, their "homework" will pay off on three ways:

- First, they will have a clearer idea of what they are passionate about.
- Second, they will gain the understanding firsthand of how to be successful in their chosen career.
- Last, their investments of time and money for a college education will be better utilized.

If young people get involved in those four steps, not only are they going to have a much stronger foundation toward pursuing ultimate success in their life, but they're also going to be in the strongest position possible for scholarship success. I think that would make them as well as their family very happy.

Wright

In your presentations, as you talk about action steps, you also say there are four essential skills for students to develop. Will you explain to us what they are and how they impact success?

Fedora

The four essential skills that every young person should strive to be an expert in are:

1. Time management skills
2. Writing skills
3. Computer skills
4. Public speaking skills

Time management—Time management is essential to master. If students improve time management, their studying and grades will improve. It will ultimately greatly enhance their life, as young people are trying to find balance in their life. Students want to be well rounded—to be involved with a sport or activity, have time for a part-time job and friends. To begin a strong habit of effective time management, students need to start using a planner or calendar to record their weekly assignments and commitments. As we all know, the older we get, the busier we become. This habit formed early can remove unnecessary stress and build personal confidence.

Writing skills—I meet teachers at hundreds of schools who ask me to emphasize to my student audiences the personal commitment they need to make to become stronger writers. Our technology has given the current generation "spell-check" and "grammar-check" and an unfortunate reliance on such tools. A student could have an idea that could change an organization or even an entire industry; but unless they're able to communicate those ideas in writing they will not get very far. I stress to students all the time that they have teachers available to them and if they know they need some additional help with writing, utilize those resources while they have them.

Computer skills—Education in technology is beginning earlier and earlier for students. I encourage my audiences to push themselves to stay at the cutting edge of their technology education. Again, I stress to students to take advantage of those teachers while they have access to them and learn as much as they possibly can.

Public speaking—The sooner students become confident communicators, the greater their edge to success over their peers becomes. I emphasize that they should get involved in their local Toastmasters group or get involved in a debate club at school to develop strong public speaking skills.

If young people take advantage of these four action steps, and if they develop these four essential skills, they will have confidence, communication skills, stronger professional etiquette, stronger understanding of what they want to do and what they don't want to do, which obviously will again be a smarter investment in time and money for their college plan. They will have a resume with substance that will catch the attention of any recruiter. Their "completed homework assignments" will have developed a well rounded, self-motivated individual who will be on a strong success path toward accomplishing clear goals and dreams.

Wright

What are the greatest obstacles that students face?

Fedora

The biggest obstacles are what I call the "what ifs." What if I don't succeed? What if I'm not smart enough? What if I can't get a job doing what I want to do? What if I can't afford college? What if I'm shy? There are many of us—adults as well as students—who share these obstacles. The "what if obstacles" are fears. These fears can keep us from the success we desire. When faced with the "what if obstacles," students need to take control and face their fears square on. Ask "what if I *do* succeed?" "What if I *am* smart enough?" etc.

If we can take a successful step and push through that fear, those "what if obstacles" now become opportunities to build self-motivation, self-empowerment and ultimately a successful life.

Wright

How did you become an expert on success for young people?

Fedora

My own success journey began with my first internship at age sixteen. That first internship eventually led to a total of six internships at the time I graduated from college. On the day of graduation I looked around and realized that each and every student who was there was picking up the same "piece of paper"—their degree. I, however, had a second piece of paper—a resume that related to what I wanted to do with my life. That resume was full of experience and ultimately placed me in a powerful position over my peers. While they were trying to "find any job," I had multiple job offers. I was able to ask for a larger starting salary and I was positioned to design my life.

Students can place themselves in the same powerful position—if they start early.

Wright

What does your company, Edge to Success Enterprises, LLC, do to help students succeed?

Fedora

I founded Edge to Success Enterprises, LLC, to bring motivational messages to students and help them be proactive rather than reactive. The biggest mistake I see out there is that students are waiting for their parents, teachers, and counselors to tell them what to do. I want to let students know that they can take the reins themselves if they're willing to do that "homework," if they're willing to take the steps, if they're willing to push through their fear. If they are proactive they can really design their own life.

Wright

What final thoughts do you have regarding young people pursuing success?

Fedora

Let me tell you a story. This has to do with a young person who has done exactly what I'm suggesting that students do to be successful—be proactive.

Last summer I was asked to speak during an event in the Bronx in New York City. I met a guidance counselor who told me about her niece who was a senior last year. Her niece applied for almost two hundred scholarships. Why did she apply for that many? Out of thousands of students I meet every year, I've never even heard of someone who has won every single scholarship he or she had applied for. This girl decided to do as much as she could do. By the time she was walking down that aisle, picking up her high school diploma, she had about two hundred scholarship applications in the mailbox. Everyone wants to know how many she actually won; but that's the wrong question. The question should be how much money did that girl get? She got close to $80,000 in scholarship money, which was ultimately more than what she needed for her bachelor's degree and she was able to put some of that money toward her future master's degree.

Students should be willing to take a few steps—a few minutes—each day, whether it is to get involved in a club, get involved by doing an internship, get involved in community service, or get on a computer and start researching scholarships. If they're willing to do this "life homework" they can transform their lives and become extremely successful in whatever it is they choose to do. Young people need to recognize that they have the greatest edge to success if they use it wisely—*time*. By starting early they can accelerate their path to a success-filled life. But this "life homework" for students requires personal commitment, hard work, and desire. The "assignments" can be completed when a student makes the personal choice to get the job done.

Wright

What an interesting conversation, especially for me since I've got one going into college within the next year.

Fedora

David, I've enjoyed this and I wish your daughter the best of luck. I hope you will encourage her to get on the ball, especially with the scholarships.

Wright

We're doing that already but there are a lot of things you've mentioned that I had no idea about. I've learned something here and I'm sure our readers will as well.

Today we've been talking with Jean Fedora. She is the founder and CEO of Edge to Success Enterprises. Her company presents motivational and entertaining presentations to high school and college students. As we have found today, she knows a lot about essential skills and action steps that young people can take to be successful in their career and in their life.

Jean, thank you so much for being with us today on *Speaking of Success.*

About the Author

JEAN FEDORA jump-started her career in the entertainment industry as an intern for New York City talent agencies and casting offices. After graduating from Wagner College she became one of the youngest talent managers in New York at age twenty-two. She has helped launch the careers of young actors into television, film, and Broadway. She has spoken throughout the United States both for the entertainment industry and for the education industry helping thousands of young people create plans of action to achieve their goals. In 2006 she founded Edge to Success Enterprises, LLC, a company that delivers motivational presentations to thousands of students each year with the help of corporate sponsorship. She is currently a graduate student at New York University's Public Relations and Corporate Communications Masters program.

Jean Fedora
Edge to Success Enterprises, LLC
P.O. BOX 192
Maplewood, NJ 07040
Phone: 866.802.3112
Fax: 973.447.0514
E-mail: info@edge2success.com
www.edge2success.com

Chapter 15

GREG GUDORF

THE INTERVIEW

David Wright (Wright)

Today we're talking with Gregory D. Gudorf. His career stretches over thirty years of consumer electronics marketing, sales, and business development activities. As a teenager in a television and appliance store started by his grandfather in 1946, Greg learned the basics of serving the consumer and operating a small business first-hand. His career progressed through a variety of retail, distribution, and manufacturing organizations including nearly ten years with Sony Electronics where he last served as Vice President of Television Marketing. Having traveled extensively, including internationally, Greg finds pleasure in meeting people of all cultures and exploring differences as well as similarities in varied approaches to life and business.

Greg, welcome to *Speaking of Success*.

Why is the power of "choice" such an important element of your views toward success?

Gregory Gudorf (Gudorf)

Personal choice is the over-arching key to success. Yes, you can choose to accept success or not. The simple fact is that each of us always has a choice to make in our personal sphere, our relationships with others, in our career aspirations, and in what we deem success to be. Choice is a source of power that is far too often ignored or even bemoaned as if it didn't exist. Have you ever heard someone say I would be successful "except"? Their exceptions are many. Success would be theirs except they are too old, too young, too short, too tall, too fat, too skinny, too educated, too under-educated, too poor, or too rich (yes, you can be rich and still not be successful). According to such thinking, everything they do "except" some nagging element (usually an element seemingly beyond their control) is aligned against their success and so they struggle. In fact, it is because of that one exception that they cannot achieve the desired outcome and so success is deemed to be out of reach. All of these exceptions make for good rationalization material but none of them carry the real secret of success.

Wright

Given the struggle associated with exceptions and rationalizations, how do you push past them toward success?

Gudorf

Everything we do boils down to the choices we make including whether or not we choose to accept success. It may be easier to point to other circumstances that seem to leave us with "no choice" but to do so is to err, as there is always a choice to be made. Granted, sometimes the options in front of us are not ones we would wish to choose from but they are choices and therefore we have some form of control over situations even if our first instinct is otherwise. Believing in choice and recognizing the inherent power in exercising our choice is an important foundation step on the path to success. If one of the choices we make is to accept success we will find success.

I believe the secret to success lies in choosing to accept success, and the word "accept" itself holds the keys to unlocking the power of that choice. The keys to success lie in Always Considering Communication, Education, Persistence, and Thrift (ACCEPT).

Wright

So "accept" forms an acronym, ACCEPT, for which the first consideration you suggest is Communication. Why is communication such an important consideration?

Gudorf

The word "communication" means: *the exchange of thoughts, messages, or information, as by speech, signals, writing, or behavior.*

I used to think that the secret to success was to hone one's sales skills. At an early age and growing up with a father who was a traveling salesman, I saw sales skills as one of the key skill sets of success. In fact, the most valuable sales lesson I ever garnered occurred when my father would make me wait before I was allowed to go door-to-door selling candies to the neighborhood as part of a Cub Scout fundraiser. The reason I had to wait was because he required I practice my sales presentation in front of him to make sure it was up to snuff for the neighbors.

His simple presentation training taught me to start my sales communication with a proper introduction, followed by fully describing the features being offered (rich chocolate candies with nutty caramel flavors), then the benefit derived via funding the scouting effort, and finally to close the sale. While it proved wildly successful in moving the needle on candy sales, it wasn't until much later that I realized my father's little presentation exercise was really a lesson in the power of clear and direct communication.

A person's ability to communicate clearly and succinctly in the business and personal relationships of day-to-day life will determine how far that person will go on his or her quest for success far more accurately than nearly any other factor. Communication is truly a key to success.

Communication also happens to be such a common function that most of us don't give it another thought until we become aware of real communication troubles and then we tend to blame the other party! From the time we were babies we learned how to express our needs and wants and thus began our understanding of communication. However, the art of communication goes much beyond simply expressing our own wants and needs. As the dictionary says, communication is a *two-way* exchange of thoughts, messages, or information using a wide variety of delivery methods including speech, behavior, and body language.

Wright

What are some good tactics for people seeking to improve their communication abilities?

Gudorf

As it relates to any quest for success, you need to search for guideposts to get and keep things moving on the desired track. Personally, I had the luck of being introduced to speech, debate, and *Roberts Rules of Order* (for the proper management of meetings) via the Future Farmers of America. Surprised? So was I. When I joined the FFA as a high-school student I had no idea that such skill set training made up part of their curriculum. What a blessing the FFA turned out to be as a venue for learning and practicing the basics of public communication skills. We should all encourage young people to seek such opportunity and to embrace it wherever and whenever they find it.

As an adult, one of the most effective opportunities available for honing personal communication skills is to join Toastmasters. Founded in 1924, The Toastmasters organization is focused on "making effective communication a reality." It's been said that the fear of public speaking ranks just above the fear of death in most people's mind. With such a strong stigma of fear attached to it, one might rightfully ask how public speaking could help foster better communication skills and thus lead to success.

The good news here is that communication is truly a skill that can be learned. As such, the process of preparing, practicing, and then reviewing the results is a winning combination for building the skills of communication. Toastmasters provides a forum for learning and practicing these skills in a safe, supportive, and truly low-cost environment. It accomplishes this through a process whereby each member builds his or her skill sets while working through a series of speeches designed to build confidence and enable a member to move from a simple introductory speech to a complete presentation. What's more, because there are no "teachers," the support of the group (along with the Toastmasters' principles) is what guides the learning experience.

I've personally seen the transformational power inherent in Toastmasters participation. The Toastmasters club at Sony Electronics in San Diego was a start-up club I was personally involved in witnessing take on life. That club showcased a group of co-workers as they moved from nervous and fearful to ever more confident and poised as they worked through their first few Toastmasters speaking exercises. Not only did participants enjoy improvements in their communication skills, but because the clubs are not led by outsiders, the members themselves had a chance to stretch their leadership wings in the act of nurturing the club along and facilitating the necessary elements for any growing organization.

If you don't think you have time for an ongoing, weekly, one-hour club commitment, consider a two-day, hands-on seminar of the type the Ziglar Performance Group enables via their Essential Presentation Skills seminar. Having recently witnessed ten co-workers proceed through the experience and report very positive results, I can attest to the power of such programs. Do make sure, however, that you find a session that stresses the hands-on aspect of the practice, preferably with video taping of the participants. Video taping is an important ingredient, and actually seeing your performance is when your communication skill set is truly honed. And remember, in communication skill building, as with so many other skill exercises, you are never really done practicing.

Whether you choose to join Toastmasters or to pursue other forms of communication skill building, when you fully consider communications in your quest for success, your chances of achieving your desired outcome will rise dramatically.

Wright

Education is often thought of as something only necessary through high school and college years. What ongoing role does it play in long-term success beyond a passage into adulthood and one's initial real-world job?

Gudorf

The definition of "education" is: *The act or process of educating or being educated; the knowledge or skill obtained or developed by a learning process; an instructive or enlightening experience.*

Consider education when you find yourself struggling to achieve success. What additional education—in what form—could make the difference between exasperation and success? Education comes in formal and informal buckets. Both are necessary in today's world.

As one who took eleven years to achieve a bachelor's degree and three more for an MBA, I can relate to the difficulties of pursuing the formal part of an education while dealing with day-to-day life. There's always something that seems to stand in the way. Often those obstacles resist until the point where one says, "Geez, if I start now, I'll be so old by the time I finish I shouldn't even bother to start." A good response is always, "Well, how old will you be in a few years if you don't start now!" Formal education may seem like a tough goal to chase, and it is, but that doesn't lessen the value or importance of accepting the challenge.

Today's employers require ever greater levels of formal education, in large part because the pool of candidates you're competing with is much better educated. According to the Nebraska Council on Economic Education, between 1971 and 1990 the percentage of the population in the United States of those who had completed four or more years of college doubled to more than 21 percent, and that trend has not slowed since. What's more, the earning power of a person with five or more years of college was nearly two and a half times greater than that of someone with just three or less years of high school. Additionally, as our country's economy continues to move toward the much heralded "information economy," manual-labor-only careers become less and less a percentage of the overall economic value from which to earn financial success.

If funding is a barrier to pursuing more formal education, don't overlook an employer as a potential source of those funds. The worst your employer can say if you ask is no, and he or she might just say yes and agree to fund your need. And employers should remember that the only thing worse than training employees and losing them is perhaps *not* training them and keeping them!

Wright

What about the idea that any learning is good learning?

Gudorf

Well, the debate continues as to whether or not education of any type is valuable versus education solely focused on the needs of the employer. My own opinion is that it is the learning process or enlightening experience itself that counts the most. Something I learned that might seemingly have little direct implication on my job performance is still a process and a discipline learned or refreshed that should prove applicable in some way in the work environment. Both employers and employees should be interested in the benefits of furthering education on all fronts.

Of course, formal education alone is not the whole story. Many of the best lessons are only realized in the process of doing as opposed to studying. And sometimes it takes both in an informal setting to really teach and learn. Several years back while working to help launch the SonyStyle Web site (www.sonystyle.com) I realized as a business manager that I needed to better understand, at least at a minimal level, the view from the engineering perspective as to how Web sites were built. To that end, I took a week's vacation, bought a copy of *HTML 4 Dummies,* and proceeded to build my very own personal Web site, which has evolved and can be visited today at www.gudorf.net.

My wife thought it crazy for me to spend a week's vacation sequestered away in our computer room but the resulting process of creating a personal Web site, regardless of how crude that first site turned out, proved to be a very valuable education exercise for me personally as well as for my employer at the time, Sony Electronics. What's more, that little bit of informal learning has served me well, as that first Web site has developed over the years into a family and personal tool that has brought much pleasure in return. Could I truly, directly relate with the intricacies of engineering a massive Web site from studying and practicing with *HTML 4 Dummies* as my guide? No, but I did increase my understanding of an issue that was a drag on my quest for a successful project launch, and that is informal education at its best!

The process of education doesn't stop when the formal path appears to have reached an endpoint. The joy of informal learning can pay huge dividends on a personal fulfillment front for many years beyond the practical reason for its pursuit.

It's really a matter of continual education and the mindset that goes with it that can often unlock the success desired. In today's world, access to continuing education is greater than ever, including a large number of formats from which to choose: in class, live seminars, and even online programs. And while each approach serves the many different ways we each prefer to learn, find the combinations that work for you and choose to pursue your success through education.

Wright

So far we've discussed the idea of always considering communication and education as keys to success. The next letter in your acronym ACCEPT stands for Persistence. Please tell us why.

Gudorf

The definition of persistence is: *The act of persisting; refusing to give up or let go; persevering obstinately.*

Once you have the foundational blocks of success, communication, and education well underway, you're probably already starting to feel and realize some level of success. Beware! Don't slow up now, as you'll surely learn first-hand that persistence is required to achieve true success.

Zig Ziglar often tells a story that is a model lesson in the need for persistence. It seems these two fellows were out for a long drive in the country on a sweltering, hot, humid day in a car that had no air conditioning. As luck would have it, they came across an old-fashioned roadside rest area. I say "old-fashioned" because it did not have vending machines and running water as today's modern rest stops do. This rest area featured porta-potties, an old hand-pump, and ground well for drinking water. One of the fellows spied the pump and immediately went to work pumping the handle up and down, up and down in an effort to bring forth a cool refreshing drink of water. As the task of pumping went from a few strokes to a few minutes of effort in the hot sun with sweat beginning to pour down his brow ever faster, he felt certain the pump must be on top of a dry well and promptly stopped pumping.

His friend immediately jumped up grabbed the handle, started pumping again, and exclaimed to his friend that if you just stop pumping, all that cool refreshing water working its way to the surface will merely drop back down without the persistent pressure of the pump. And so, the friend took up the task of pushing that pump handle down and pulling it back up over and over for several more minutes. In time, water started to gush forward—water that was cool, clear, and exactly what was desired to quench the thirst of both fellows. They enjoyed their success. What's more, once the water began to flow, the task of keeping it flowing became much easier because, as long as persistent pumping was exerted, the water would keep flowing forth from the well. Their task had become easier when success was achieved but the necessity of persisting, first with full labor and then at a reduced level of labor, was the key to their continuing to enjoy the fruits of that success.

Do you know the saying that the longest journey begins with a first step? Think of the need for persistence in the context of such a journey. If you set out for a distant destination, you usually have a prescribed trail or methodology in mind, and you know that if you but persist on your trek you will nearly always reach that destination. Along the way you have to contend with the lure of instant gratification in the form of tempting rest spots, interesting side trips, and more. While you can certainly partake of each of these temptations, it is only if you ultimately persist towards your destination that you will succeed in reaching it.

Wright

Will you give us a real-world, everyday example of persistence?

Gudorf

I enjoy day-hikes in the mountains whenever chance allows. I'll often set my sights on a viewpoint in pursuit of an expansive vista or perhaps a soothing waterfall. Sometimes the trails are more difficult than imagined. Sometimes the weather is worse than expected. Sometimes it is just plain hunger, cold, heat, or fatigue that pleads with my every footstep forward to stop and rest or worse yet, to turn around without reaching the destination. Since turning back is not an option, I like to consider that it becomes a game of carefully measuring which sidesteps to take versus how long it will delay my continuing forward effort to finally reach the viewpoint. A hiker knows from experience that the end result will almost always be worth the irritants along the way, and that's why persistence carries the day.

Here's an example any fellow traveler will relate to. A modern day traveler works through the same troubles plaguing persistence when the airport security line is long, the airplane is departing late, the weather is bad, the plane changes to a longer, slower course, the luggage takes forever to arrive at the destination, etc. And yet, travelers persist in their journey because they understand that only through persistence will they reach their final destination. Imagine what would happen if our goals for success were served with the same persistence as our desire to get to O'Hare or wherever our plane's destination might be!

The power of persistence has proved itself time and again in all endeavors. We struggle so hard against having to persist due to the lure of instant gratification. True success never comes instantly. Remember that when the media speaks of an "overnight success" you can bet that the person has worked long and hard, persisting through hours, months, and often years of effort to achieve "overnight success" status.

Don't give up on your success just shy of its full realization due to a lack of persistence. If you do, you'll remain hot and thirsty without the cool drink of water you need to continue and without ever achieving your desired success.

Wright

The last letter in the acronym ACCEPT stands for thrift. That's a term not often associated with success. Please explain.

Gudorf

The definition of thrift is: *Wise economy in the management of money and other resources; frugality.*

Always consider thrift in any quest for success. In today's world where credit is so easy to obtain and consumerism and the consumption it promotes so widespread, the old fashioned value of thrift is not often considered a key element or secret of success. No one wants to talk about budgets and spending less than you make. In fact, according to an article by Lena Sherrod in the July 2004 edition of *Essence* magazine, it is estimated that some 60 million Americans have no savings and thus by definition live paycheck to paycheck. These aren't just low-income earners either, as nearly one third of those 60 million earn $75,000 or more annually.

Breaking the paycheck-to-paycheck habit may not be easy, but it is a straightforward prospect. It requires understanding the value of a budget and sticking to it in a manner that rewards delayed gratification.

My mother taught me the value of thrift when I was about twelve years of age. With a budding cash flow from my little paper route and a big desire for a brand new bicycle, she helped me establish a simple envelope-based budgeting system. The system had one envelope for long-term savings, one for charity, and one for short-term use. My favorite envelope quickly became the one earmarked for short-term use, as that was what would fund the purchase of my shiny new bicycle before that first summer faded into fall.

What's more important, however, is that the process of regularly adding to those envelopes and watching the amounts accumulate until I had enough to realize my dream underscored the need for thrift in action.

I recall being in a large room full of sales and marketing folks early in my career when the seminar leader casually asked for a show of hands as to how many people arrived at the seminar that day in a Mercedes, Jaguar, BMW, or other luxury automobile. A fair number of hands went up with a rush of pride. The leader then asked if a Chevrolet wouldn't have done just as well in getting them to the seminar while leaving a substantial number of dollars still in their bank accounts. Suddenly, those raised hands wavered a bit sheepishly.

Now, don't get me wrong. I love the ride of a BMW or other fine automobile as much, if not more than the next person. However, partaking of such prototypical success status symbols before you've achieved the lasting success that can afford them is a sure way to lengthen the task time required before you can enjoy the true fruits of success. It's been said that one of the anti-thriftiest scents in the world is the wonderfully seductive aroma of a brand new automobile. Thrift would remind you that a nearly new used car will have already suffered through the greatest degree of depreciation and still deliver the experience desired sans a bit of that expensive new car scent.

Given that the consumer drives our society on so many fronts and the notion of consumption is often so closely linked with proclaiming to the world your success, thrift can be a difficult habit to cultivate. However, is it really success if you're driving that fine automobile during the day, but lying awake at night wondering how you're going to afford the basic household expenses?

An old-line sales manager used to tell me that he wanted his sales team to drive big, fancy new automobiles. When I asked why, he replied that nothing kept a sales team hard at work selling like having to face a big monthly payment for an automobile. Yes, he saw the downside of not being thrifty in such a major purchase, and put it to work for him at the expense of his sales team's ultimate success.

Wright

We hear much about "easy" credit nowadays. How does that work against the suggestion of thrift?

Gudorf

According to the PBS *Frontline* segment titled "The Secret History of The Credit Card," 144 million Americans have credit cards and collectively charged $1.5 trillion in purchases in 2004. That staggering number alone is of course not proof of a lack of thrift among the American public because the ability to use credit cards has now become nearly ubiquitous. What's more, the fact that 55 million of those users manage to pay off their credit card balance entirely each and every month indicates that many folks use credit cards responsibly, at least from a debt management perspective. However, do those 55 million users make their purchases with thrift in mind or are they more apt to purchase on the spur of the moment given the ease with which their credit cards facilitate such purchases? Even smart debt managers may not be thrifty.

And what about the other nearly 90 million credit card holders who do not pay off their monthly charge balances? Those folks are paying substantive amounts of interest to float that debt. According to the Motley Fool (www.fool.com) a favorite personal finance service with a motto that says they promise "to educate, amuse, and enrich," in 2001 alone, Americans paid a total $50 billion in credit card finance charges. Forget for a moment whether or not the purchases that drove such a large finance charge were thrifty purchases, there is little potential for rationalizing $50 billion in finance charges as a thrifty expenditure. In 2001 $50 billion spent otherwise would have purchased, free and clear, about 232,000 average homes or funded jobs paying $50,000 in annual salary for one million people that year.

The reality of thrift is generally rooted in the small purchases that no one pays attention to until the total impact grows to a shocking cost. Without considering thrift in the day-to-day reality of life, success can become ever more elusive in spite of best intentions. One of the surest ways to speed forth the joy of success is through liberal applications of thrift. Whether you're working your way up the ladder of life or already enjoying the fruits of your labor, the longevity of your success can be greatly enhanced with a keen eye toward choosing thrift.

Wright

Now that we understand how the power of choice when applied in conjunction with the acronym ACCEPT (Always Consider Communication, Education, Persistence and Thrift) can help guide us on the path to success, do you have any other thoughts in this regard?

Gudorf

I truly believe the secret to success is to make the choice to accept success. Don't concentrate on the exceptions that seem to stand in your way. Rather, concentrate on accepting success and then always consider communication, education, persistence, and thrift and you'll find the needed keys that will unlock the success you desire. After all, it is your choice to make. There is only the need to choose, and then choose again, until your success is in hand.

As Zig Ziglar is fond of saying, we were each "designed for accomplishment, engineered for success, and endowed with the seeds of greatness." Choose wisely. Choose to accept success.

As my grandfather, Norbert H. Gudorf wrote many years ago, "Everybody is born with some God-given talents. To recognize those talents and to put them into practice is a formula for a successful life, not measured necessarily in worldly possessions, but in the satisfaction of having been involved in helping your fellow citizens enjoy a more fruitful life and in rewarding your Creator for having given you the opportunity and the talents to do this. Always keep in mind the simple fact that there are only two things you can take with you when you pass from this life to your eternal home—what you have done for the honor and glory of your Creator and what you have done for your fellow citizens."

In closing, and to paraphrase an old saying, simply choose to go as far as you can see and then you'll see further choices for you to consider. When you choose to accept success, you will be choosing to achieve success.

About the Author

Greg Gudorf currently serves as Chief Operating Officer of Digeo, Inc., a developer of digital video recorder products for the cable and consumer electronics industries based in Seattle, Washington. Greg often speaks at industry events, holds multiple patents in the consumer electronics arena, and has been published in industry magazines and periodicals. He is a member of the National Speakers Association and also enjoys working with the Ziglar Performance Group helping individuals and teams achieve their maximum potential.

Greg Gudorf
E-mail: greg@gudorf.net
www.gudorf.net
Blog: www.gudorfgroup.com

Chapter 16

James D. Jackson

THE INTERVIEW

David Wright (Wright)

Today we're talking with James D. Jackson. James is one of the most sought after professional speakers on the planet. He is the owner of James D. Jackson Enterprises and Regal Publishing, Inc. He is an expert in the fields of academic improvement, corporate training, book publishing, movie production, and life insurance. His seminars include "Release the Genius in You" for students, "Operating in the Black" for business restructuring, and "One Time Closer" for sales professionals. You can find all you need to know about him by logging onto www.Jamesdjackson.com.

James, welcome to *Speaking of Success.*

James D. Jackson (Jackson)

Thank you.

Wright

How do you define success?

Jackson

Well, I define success as setting a goal and then accomplishing that goal no matter what it takes to do that.

Wright

So, in one word, what quality must someone possesses to become successful?

Jackson

Perseverance. I define perseverance as doing something over and over while failing at it until you ultimately succeed.

Wright

Even while you are failing at it?

Jackson

That's right.

Wright

So, what type of people should you surround yourself with?

Jackson

People who share your vision.

Wright

What about mentors?

Jackson

I think they are a must. Find someone who has done exactly what it is that you want to do, and emulate them.

Wright

So what in your opinion stops people from becoming successful?

Jackson

I think everyone has a stroke of genius in them. People don't succeed because they let others talk them out of their great ideas.

Wright

Is that manifested by low self-image?

Jackson

Without a doubt.

Wright

So what you are saying is that we all have within us everything we need to be successful and all we have to do is mine it.

Jackson

We all have within us the ability to attract people who have strengths where we have weaknesses.

Wright

So how do I create success then?

Jackson

By surrounding yourself with people who typically have strengths where you have weaknesses. All good companies or corporations are great because they hire people who compliment the others on the team.

Wright

What about networking?

Jackson

Your network determines your net worth. Surround yourself with as many affluent people as you can—it's bound to rub off.

Wright

Do you believe that success is based on a concentration of power?

Jackson

Yes I do. I think we often try to do more than one thing at a time. If we just focus most of our attention (if not all of our attention) on one thing at a time, I'm sure we would be more successful.

Wright

In the last two or three years, all I hear about is multitasking. How can we concentrate on just one thing when our employers are asking us to multitask?

Jackson

Complete one thing at a time as quickly as you can and immediately get started on the next project.

Wright

So by concentrating you mean that all of your thoughts should be with some particular goal in mind?

Jackson

Exactly.

Wright

In the last several years we have seen people making millions of dollars, running major corporations, responsible for all kinds of employees, and they are going to jail and their character is being questioned. Is character a big component of success?

Jackson

Yes it is.

Wright

How do you think character develops? For some of us who didn't have the greatest childhood in the world, how does one develop character?

Jackson

By trying to do everything that you know that's morally and ethically right all the time. If you do it as often as you can, hopefully it will then define you and you can make great things happen throughout your life.

Wright

Do you agree that in this day and time your word still should be your bond?

Jackson

I agree. I think that's the most important thing. If you tell people this is what you are going to do and you do it, they will look to you in the future as someone they can trust.

Wright

I remember reading some things you had written about that happened about three years ago—a friend needed some money to pay a utility bill or something. Do you remember that?

Jackson

I do.

Wright

What happened?

Jackson

Well, he fell behind on some bills and he asked for one thing and I will always remember: under-promise and over-deliver. He needed one bill paid, but I also looked into the refrigerator and noticed there was no food. Instead of asking about the money for food, I just added the money and put a note that read, "Buy some food for yourself while you're at it." That same person has referred countless clients to me.

Wright

Maybe that is the "extra mile" they talk about in the Bible.

Jackson

That's right.

Wright

Many people equate success with money. What professions would you suggest people enter if they want to make a lot of money?

Jackson

I would say any profession where they do not have a cap on the amount of money they can make, whether it be the entertainment business, insurance, or opening your own business. But then again, I know a lot of school teachers and others who have a capped salary. Obviously it will be very difficult for them to make a lot of money, so they would need to find a profession where there is no ceiling on how much money they can actually make.

Wright

Commission sales?

Jackson
That would be a good one.

Wright
I wonder why people run from commission sales.

Jackson
People typically don't want to work hard. They want to have just enough money to pay their bills. Sales can be the easiest, lowest paying profession, or the hardest, highest paying profession. It just depends on whether you are going to work hard or not.

Wright
As a successful business owner, what advice would you give to our readers who are considering starting a business?

Jackson
I would find out all of the information I could about the company I wanted to open. Preferably try to find one that has low overhead if you can do that. Hire competent people, and collectively, with all employees doing their jobs, your business will be around for many years to come.

Wright
So, knowing that you're a goal-setter and that you get things done, what is next on the horizon for James D. Jackson? What plans do you have for the next few years?

Jackson
Well, right now I want to make independent films. It's much easier to get your message across through the television or the movie screen.

Wright
Where are you going to shoot the movies?

Jackson
Right here in Atlanta.

Wright
That's interesting. You are still on the move.

Jackson

That's right.

Wright

Well, what an interesting conversation. I've learned a lot here this afternoon. I know our readers will also learn as they read this chapter. I want to tell you how much I appreciate your spending all this time with me answering these questions.

Jackson

You're welcome.

Wright

Today we have been speaking with James D. Jackson. He is an expert in the fields of academic improvement, corporate training, book publishing, and life insurance. He has completed a film director's course and is now making movies. You can find all you need to know about him by logging onto www.Jamesdjackson.com.

About the Author

James D. Jackson is one of the most sought after professional speakers on the planet. He is the owner of James D. Jackson enterprises and Regal Publishing, Inc. He is an expert in the fields of academic improvement, corporate training, book publishing, and life insurance. His seminars include "Release the Genius in You" for students, "Operating in the Black" for business restructuring, and "One Time Closer" for sales professionals. Log onto www.Jamesdjackson.com to learn more.

James D. Jackson Enterprises
2850 Delk Rd. Suite 6-A
Marietta, Georgia 30067
www.jamesdjackson.com